# I Can Beat Anorexia!

*by the same author*

**I Can Beat Obesity!**
**Finding the Motivation, Confidence and Skills to Lose Weight and Avoid Relapse**
*Dr Nicola Davies*
*Foreword by Jane DeVille-Almond*
ISBN 978 1 78592 153 7
eISBN 978 1 78450 420 5

**Eating Disorder Recovery Handbook**
**A Practical Guide to Long-Term Recovery**
*Dr Nicola Davies and Emma Bacon*
ISBN 978 1 78592 133 9
eISBN 978 1 78450 398 7

*of related interest*

**Rebalance Your Relationship with Food**
**Reassuring recipes and nutritional support for positive, confident eating**
*Emma Bacon*
ISBN 978 1 78592 119 3
eISBN 978 0 85701 278 4

**Beating Eating Disorders Step by Step**
**A Self-Help Guide for Recovery**
*Anna Paterson*
ISBN 978 1 84310 340 0
eISBN 978 1 84642 759 6

**Can I Tell You about Eating Disorders?**
**A Guide for Friends, Family and Professionals**
*Bryan Lask and Lucy Watson*
*Illustrated by Fiona Field*
ISBN 978 1 84905 421 8
eISBN 978 0 85700 797 1
Can I tell you about...? series

# I Can Beat Anorexia!

Finding the Motivation, Confidence and
Skills to Recover and Avoid Relapse

DR NICOLA DAVIES

Foreword by Deanne Jade

Jessica Kingsley *Publishers*
London and Philadelphia

Copyright acknowledgements are listed on page 14.

First published in 2017
by Jessica Kingsley Publishers
73 Collier Street
London N1 9BE, UK
and
400 Market Street, Suite 400
Philadelphia, PA 19106, USA

www.jkp.com

**Library of Congress Cataloging in Publication Data**
Names: Davies, Nicola (Health psychologist)
Title: I can beat anorexia! : finding the motivation, confidence and skills
   to recover and avoid relapse / Dr. Nicola Davies.
Description: London ; Philadelphia : Jessica Kingsley Publishers, 2017.
Identifiers: LCCN 2016056332 | ISBN 9781785921872 (alk. paper)
Subjects: LCSH: Anorexia nervosa--Treatment. | Anorexia
   nervosa--Psychological aspects. | Eating disorders--Social aspects.
Classification: LCC RC552.A5 D38 2017 | DDC 616.85/262--
dc23 LC record available at https://lccn.loc.gov/2016056332

**British Library Cataloguing in Publication Data**
A CIP catalogue record for this book is available from the British Library

ISBN 978 1 78592 187 2
eISBN 978 1 78450 459 5

Printed and bound in Great Britain

*This book is dedicated to anyone struggling with anorexia and those brave enough to tackle this devastating condition so that they can finally be free of its chains.*

# Contents

# Foreword

I am honoured to write a foreword to Nicola Davies' book on behalf of the National Centre for Eating Disorders. I first met Nicola when she asked me to review her book and I was interested to see her thoughts about an illness which is so profound and which thwarts so many healers. Nicola is very special since she can contribute to our understanding of anorexia both from her experiences as a sufferer as well as from her knowledge of human motivations as a qualified Doctor in Health Psychology.

No one chooses to be anorexic; it starts with a simple and a common wish to feel better by losing a little weight. What distinguishes the anorexic from the usual dieter is their ability to withstand the pangs of extreme hunger, plus long-standing gaps in emotional resilience which would normally stop someone from losing more weight than is healthy. By the time anorexia is diagnosed, most sufferers are already entrapped, physically ill, mentally consumed with rules about eating and intense fear of weight gain, and listening exclusively to a critical voice which both encourages them to keep going while threatening retribution if they try to rebel. We experts have many explanations about anorexia, but we all agree that the illness seems 'useful' to sufferers, since it has become the only way they know to manage their feelings. That first simple wish to feel better erodes into a compulsion for continued weight loss as the sufferer's only source of self-worth, and even a 'badge of pride'.

Most sufferers come to a point of needing to escape from the clutches of anorexia, too often when the illness has done great damage to health, relationships and progress in life. But the desire to change needs to be put into action for recovery to be possible. There are many books out there which describe, in painful detail, people's eating disorder experiences; therapists need to read these to understand what anorexia is about. However, there are not many useful recovery guides and I believe that this book fills a much-needed gap. It is a great roadmap for all people with anorexia, whether stuck or actively considering change, or who have already decided that they must change but do not know how. They will still be caught in a tug of war between the desire to let go and the demands of their anorexia.

This is the worst aspect of anorexia; that each step forward invokes an equal and opposite force inviting patients back toward their illness. They have to eat when they are not hungry, ignore the shouting of the anorexic voice and experience physical changes which are unwelcome. On top of all this, they may lack preparation for the emotions and challenges of everyday life from which low weight has protected them.

The title of Nicola's book expresses her passion for change and her belief that by building up your personal strength and resources, good change will happen despite the illness fighting back. She knows full well that recovery is not just about eating more; it is feeling better about yourself so that eating is deserved and low weight no longer holds the promise of escape from pain.

Too often, therapists working with anorexia spend a lot of time searching for insight into why it happened. This is not enough. People need to grow into their own skin, take back their lives and replace the malignant control structures of anorexia with better ones. I would certainly recommend this book to people with anorexia, whatever the stage of their condition and, particularly, to people seeking recovery on their own. This book will also be useful for therapists working with anorexia who are in desperate need of a practical toolkit to help them support people who are unable to explain their resistance to change. Nicola and I both agree that together, and with the right tools, we can beat anorexia; this book will add to our good practice.

*Deanne Jade, MBPsS; Psychologist*
*Founder, National Centre for Eating Disorders*

# Acknowledgements

I would like to say a huge Thank You to those who played a role in my long but worthwhile journey to beat disordered eating:

- My loving partner, Alex Buckley, who gave me a reason to get better and ongoing support during the most difficult of times.

- My dedicated counsellor, Marian Brindle, who provided a safe environment for me to explore my eating issues and develop the tools to beat it.

- My best friend, Sharon Thornton, whose acceptance and kindness helped me accept and be kind to myself.

- Emma Bacon, co-author of my book *Eating Disorder Recovery Handbook: A Practical Guide to Long-Term Recovery*, who was a wealth of information in terms of practical advice.

I would also like to extend my gratitude to those who facilitated my growth as a health professional, especially my PhD supervisor and friend, Professor Gail Kinman. Training as a health professional was an important component of developing my ability to now help others.

Finally, I would like to thank Jessica Kingsley Publishers, for believing in the value of this book and making it available to those who could benefit from it.

# Copyright acknowledgements

Epigraph on page 21 is reproduced from *Harry Potter and the Goblet of Fire*: Copyright © J.K. Rowling 2000, with kind permission from Bloomsbury Publishing.

Epigraphs on pages 31 and 82 are reproduced from an article by Jim Rohn, American's Foremost Business Philosopher, reprinted with permission from SUCCESSS © 2016. As a world-renowned author and success expert, Jim Rohn touched millions of lives during his 46-year career as a motivational speaker and messenger of positive life change. For more information on Jim and his popular personal achievement resources or to subscribe to the weekly Jim Rohn Newsletter, visit www.JimRohn.com or www.SUCCESS.com.

Epigraph on page 38 is from *The Perpetual Calendar of Inspiration: Old Wisdom for a New World* by Vera Nazarian, published by Norilana Books and reproduced with permission.

Epigraph on page 53 is reproduced from *Silent Kingdom* by Rachel Schade, with kind permission from the author.

Epigraph on page 67 is reproduced from *The 15 Invaluable Laws of Growth: Live Them and Reach Your Potential* by John C. Maxwell © 2012, with kind permission from Center Street/Hachette Book Group.

Epigraph on page 92 by Vironika Tugaleva is reproduced by permission of the author.

Epigraph on page 104 by Auliq-Ice is reproduced by permission of the author.

Epigraph on page 115 is from *On Becoming a Person: A Therapist's View of Psychotherapy* by Carl R. Rogers. Copyright © 1961 by Carl R. Rogers, renewed 1989 by David E. Rogers and Natalie Rogers. Used by permission of Houghton Mifflin Harcourt Publishing Company. All rights reserved.

Epigraph on page 135 by Tony Gaskins is reproduced by permission of the author.

Epigraph on page 139 is reproduced from *Keep Your Love On: Connection, Communication and Boundaries* by Danny Silk, with kind permission from Loving on Purpose.

# Disclaimer

This book has been designed for adults, males as well as females, but not children. It provides you with the tools needed to beat anorexia, but it is up to you to grasp them and use them to the best of your ability. I also urge you to seek the support of a professional while embarking on this journey. Counselling, in particular, can become a trusted ally in your journey to a healthier and happier you.

Every effort has been made to ensure that the information contained in this book is correct, but it should not in any way be substituted for medical advice. I am a health psychologist and counsellor, but readers should always consult a qualified medical practitioner before making any major changes to their diet or physical activity. Neither the author nor the publisher takes responsibility for any consequences of any decision made as a result of the information contained in this book.

While the female pronoun is used throughout this book for continuity, men suffer from anorexia too and this book will also be a useful resource for them.

# Preface

First of all, congratulations on picking up *I Can Beat Anorexia!* – because *you can beat it*, and by opening this book you are giving yourself the opportunity to do just that. I know from my own personal experience just how terrifying that first step is – to even consider taking on this powerful illness. However, just think of all the time, energy and effort you give to the anorexia – to food, weight, the scales, and to self-destructive thinking. What if you were to channel that time and energy into your recovery? Indeed, one thing I have learnt about anorexia is that it often overshadows huge strength – a strength to survive, to live, to cope. Some have described it as a slow suicide, and while it can certainly be seen as such, I liken it more to a survival mechanism. Your anorexia has helped you survive to this point and, in that sense, it has done its job. But there are better, healthier, kinder ways to help yourself through life – ways that don't just help you survive, but help you thrive. It is my hope that this book will help you to develop and use these better, healthier and kinder ways to live your life.

In *I Can Beat Anorexia!* we will take a journey of four parts:

- In Part 1, we will arm you with the knowledge to beat anorexia. I want you to understand the causes and consequences of anorexia so that you are empowered to beat it if you choose to.

- In Part 2, we will prepare to beat anorexia by exploring your readiness and confidence to take this journey.

- In Part 3, we will look at beating anorexia by taking control – of your behavioural well-being, physical well-being, psychological well-being and social well-being. These dimensions of your well-being are fundamental to beating anorexia because this isn't about your weight – it is about you as a whole person with many different facets. *You are more than your weight.*

- In Part 4, we will move beyond anorexia and start to look at how you can accept yourself and begin to focus on your future hopes and dreams.

You will also find a Part 5, which you can give to your family or carers – anyone who you would like to assist you in your recovery. These pages provide your loved ones with some key insights into how they can help you.

Each chapter will start with information and finish by going 'Over to You!' In these 'Over to You!' sections, you will be able to complete some exercises to help cement your new knowledge and move you closer to your goal of beating anorexia and, later, moving beyond anorexia. Throughout, I share my own personal experiences of what helped me beat the eating disorders that plagued me from my childhood to my early 30s.

The approach within this workbook is based on the discipline of health psychology, which uses an understanding of human emotions and behaviours to help you achieve better health and well-being. I have a doctorate in Health Psychology and have experienced first-hand its power – personally and in my work – in assisting with eating disorder recovery. I have also included components that I feel are missing from many self-help books and that I could have benefited from, such as how to distinguish hunger and fullness, how to cope with weight gain, and what to do when my head and heart want different things.

Today, I am much healthier and happier – and you can be too. I won't lie. It isn't easy. It is a tough journey that takes huge amounts of persistence and patience with yourself. But you are worth it – you deserve to be happy and healthy!

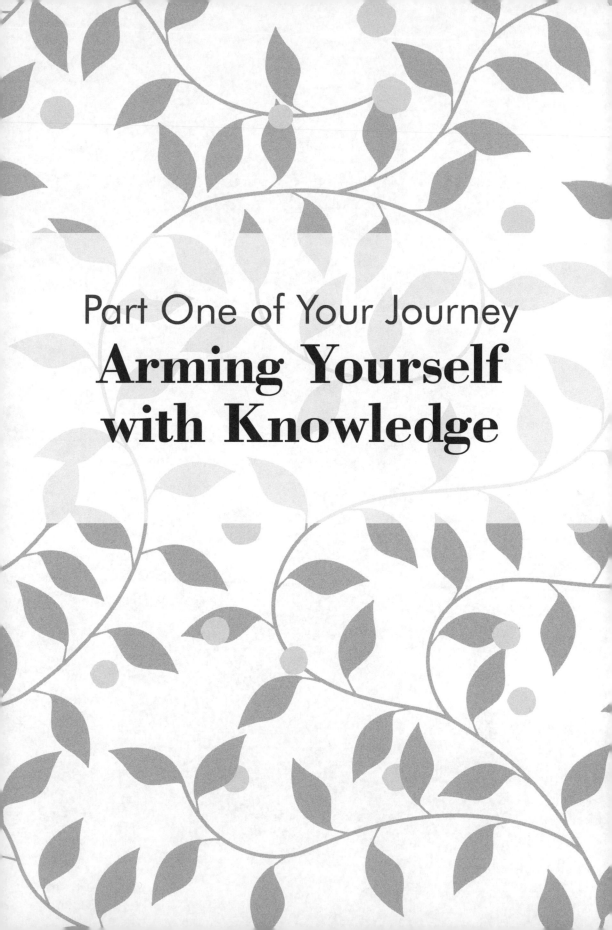

# Part One of Your Journey
# Arming Yourself with Knowledge

Chapter 1

# Understanding Anorexia

> *Understanding is the first step to acceptance, and only with acceptance can there be recovery.*
>
> J.K. Rowling

This book is about beating anorexia, but before you can do that, you need to understand it – *what* it is, *why* it is and, maybe most importantly, whether you have it. Denial is often a big part of anorexia, so it is important to step back and be objective here – to read this chapter with an open mind and to consider the very real possibility that you could have this illness. After all, something or someone has encouraged you to reach for this book.

Let's start by breaking this complex disorder down into its most basic components in order to get to know it better.

## Meet Anorexia

Anorexia enters your world like a new best friend – she is safe, reliable, strong, consistent, and there for you whenever you need her. She invests so much time and energy in you that you suddenly feel alive and in control of your life.

Yet without warning – because it is so slow and so gradual – she turns on you. She whispers in your ear:

- 'You are nothing, a no one.'

- 'You are flawed to the core.'

- 'You are worthless, such a disappointment.'

- 'Nobody likes you.'

- 'You don't deserve that.'

- 'Look at you. You are fat and disgusting. You are ugly.'

You fall deeper and deeper into a dark pit of depression, isolating yourself from others.

But then there is hope. Your friend, Anorexia, can help you. If you just listen to her attacks more closely, you will also hear the solution to your problems:

- 'Don't eat that!'

- 'Move, move, move – those calories won't budge on their own.'

- 'Stop looking at that food – it will only tempt you.'

- 'Quick, rid yourself of that meal before it is too late.'

- 'Don't even think about it; you have had your calorie allowance for the day.'

- 'Hey, why not have even less tomorrow? You'll reach your goal quicker.'

- 'Well done – another 2lb down – still a way to go though, so don't get lax.'

Before you know it, you are consumed by this dark force that you thought would protect you from the world. It is everywhere you go and everywhere you turn – in your head, in your eyes and in your heart. You literally hear, see and feel this never-ending drive for thinness and perfection. Part of you wants out, but it is too late and you have pushed everyone away. So, you give yourself over to the one thing that you do have – anorexia.

## What Is Anorexia?

Some experts believe that anorexia nervosa (referred to throughout this book as anorexia) is an eating disorder characterised by:

- the pursuit or maintenance of an extremely low body weight that is less than 85% expected for someone of your age and height

- an intense fear of and resistance to gaining weight, despite being underweight

- a distorted perception of your weight and body shape, with emphasis on evaluating yourself based on your own perception of your weight.[1]

Note here that anorexia isn't just about being underweight; it is also about the pursuit of being underweight. So, you don't have to be underweight to have anorexia. This is a myth. It takes time for someone to become underweight as a result of their anorexia-related behaviours. The illness is also a mindset. Indeed, some experts believe it is a form of 'monomania' – an emotional disorder whereby the person becomes fixated with one idea. In the case of anorexia, the fixation might be weight loss, a number on the weighing scale or the ability to say 'no' to food.

There are two main types of anorexia, both of which are driven by a distorted body image and fear of weight gain:

- **Restricting type:** Someone with restricting anorexia will severely limit the quantity of food they eat, and their calorie intake will be well below the body's requirements. They also carry out ritualistic and obsessive compulsive behaviours in relation to food and weight, such as excessive exercise, eating only at certain times or arranging food in a particular way. They are effectively slowly starving.

- **Binge/purge type:** Someone with binge/purge anorexia also severely restricts their food and calorie intake, but at times also engages in binge eating followed by purging behaviours. Purging behaviours include self-induced vomiting, excessive exercise and laxative, diuretic and enema use, or anything else that is used to compensate for the food eaten. While this might sound like the eating disorder known as bulimia nervosa, it is distinct in that the person with binge/purge anorexia is usually underweight, while the person with bulimia can be normal weight. The person with bulimia also tends to eat normally between binge/purge episodes. This book will be helpful for some aspects of bulimia recovery, such as overcoming purging behaviours, but it has been written specifically with anorexia in mind. Use this book for areas where it can help you, but do also seek help specific to bulimia. Organisations that can help you find the support you need are listed in the appendix.

## How Common Is Anorexia?

It has been estimated that over 1.6 million people in the UK are affected by an eating disorder, 10% of whom have anorexia. This equates to 1 in 100 women experiencing this type of eating disorder. While eating disorders tend to affect mainly females, they do also affect men – 11% of the estimated 1.6 million are male. The condition often affects those who are 14–25 years old, but is increasingly being diagnosed in children and older adults.[2]

## When Is a Diagnosis Made?

A diagnosis of anorexia is made when body weight is at least 15% below what is expected of someone of a particular age, gender and height, or if their body mass index (BMI) measurement is below 17.5.[3] BMI is calculated using weight and height to determine if someone is overweight or underweight for their height. However, remember – anorexia doesn't make you underweight straight away. So, even though you might only be diagnosed once you are underweight, you can be struggling with the condition before that time.

A BMI of between 15 and 17.5 indicates a mild to moderate case of anorexia as long as the condition is stable and there is low risk of rapid deterioration. A BMI of less than 15 is considered a severe case, but can still be successfully treated with support. In very severe cases, however, someone with anorexia might be admitted to hospital until weight loss can be stabilised and other serious health concerns addressed.

Although BMI is of some use for identifying anorexia, it is rather limited and can lead to cases of the illness being missed. For example, two individuals of the same height and weight, and thus the same BMI, could have very different body fat and muscle distribution. A serious athlete, for example, might be struggling with anorexia while maintaining a BMI greater than 17.5 due to extra muscle.[4]

## What Are the Tell-Tale Signs of Anorexia?

There are many signs and symptoms of anorexia. While any of these occurring on their own does not necessarily constitute a diagnosis, a number occurring together could be reason for concern. Read through the various tell-tale signs in the table below, ticking any that you might currently be experiencing.

## Signs and symptoms of anorexia

| Behavioural symptoms | Psychological symptoms | Physical symptoms |
| --- | --- | --- |
| ☐ Skipping meals<br>☐ Ritualistic behaviours surrounding meals, such as arranging food 'just so' on the plate or eating only one type of food<br>☐ Putting intense effort into making meals for others, but eating none of it yourself<br>☐ Repeatedly looking in mirrors to do 'body checks'<br>☐ Excessive exercise<br>☐ Vomiting and taking laxatives<br>☐ Feeling uncomfortable eating in public places<br>☐ Wearing baggy clothes<br>☐ Difficult relationships with family and friends<br>☐ Obsessive weighing | ☐ Intense fear of gaining weight<br>☐ Low self-esteem<br>☐ Mood swings<br>☐ Depression<br>☐ Anxiety and worry<br>☐ Distorted perception of weight or body shape<br>☐ Being a perfectionist<br>☐ Having an existing anxiety disorder, such as panic disorder, social anxiety or obsessive compulsive disorder | ☐ Amenorrhea (absence of a regular menstrual period or failure to begin menstruation in teenage girls)<br>☐ Extreme weight loss and gaunt appearance<br>☐ Abnormal blood counts and/or elevated liver enzymes<br>☐ Dehydration and electrolyte imbalances<br>☐ Dizziness and feeling faint<br>☐ Low blood pressure<br>☐ Constipation<br>☐ Abdominal pains<br>☐ Loss of bone and muscle mass<br>☐ Hair thinning and loss<br>☐ Feeling cold all the time<br>☐ Kidney stones and kidney failure<br>☐ Cardiac irregularities, especially bradycardia (slow heart)<br>☐ Difficulty sleeping and concentrating<br>☐ Downy hair on the body |

# What Causes Anorexia?

As with many illnesses, there is a complex interaction of predisposing and environmental factors that contribute to the development of anorexia.

- **Biological factors:** Anorexia has been linked to genetics, hormones and early puberty, as well as a history of obesity or body leanness, but other psychological, environmental and biological factors are likely to also be involved.[5]

- **Psychological factors:** Personality traits, such as perfectionism, need for control and neuroticism, are recognised as playing a large role in the development of anorexia.[6] Sexual or emotional abuse and low self-esteem can also increase vulnerability.[7]

- **Social factors:** Family history of eating disorders, depression or substance abuse, as well as family and social support problems, have been linked to anorexia.[8] Furthermore, although not shown to be a direct cause of anorexia, media images of thinness and social pressure from peers are recognised as contributing to pressures to look a certain way.[9]

It is unlikely to be one factor that has resulted in your struggle with anorexia. Whatever the key contributing factors, anorexia will have become your way of coping with life – with emotions, thoughts, people and situations.

## Over to You!

If you are reading this book, it is likely that you suspect yourself of having anorexia. Take some time to answer the following questions with a simple 'yes' or 'no'. Be completely honest with yourself; no one else needs to see your answers.

**?** Do I feel fat even though people tell me that I'm not?

☐ Yes ☐ No

**?** Am I terrified of gaining weight?

☐ Yes ☐ No

**?** Do I lie about how much I eat, or hide my eating habits from others?

☐ Yes ☐ No

**?** Are my friends or family concerned about my weight loss, eating habits or appearance?

☐ Yes ☐ No

**?** Do I diet, compulsively exercise or purge when I'm feeling overwhelmed or bad about myself or a situation?

☐ Yes ☐ No

**?** Do I feel powerful or in control when I go without food, over-exercise or purge?

☐ Yes ☐ No

**?** Do I base my self-worth on my weight or body size?

☐ Yes ☐ No

If you answered 'yes' to any of these questions, then it is likely that you have an unhealthy relationship with food and with your body. Therefore, you could be at risk of having or developing anorexia. If you answered 'yes' to all of these questions, then it is likely that you do have anorexia. In either case, the best action you can take to help yourself is to seek professional support. This book can help you in your journey to beat anorexia, but professional support is also high on the list of recovery tools, as discussed in more detail in Chapter 4. Anorexia is a serious illness and seeking professional support will empower you in your journey to beat it.

✎ Take some time to think about how you feel after answering the above questions. Maybe you are shocked? Scared? Maybe they just helped you confirm what you already knew? Perhaps you are angry or want to throw this book down? Jot down how you are feeling right now.

_____

_____

_____

_____

_____

All of these feelings and more are completely natural. Whatever you are feeling, I want to reassure you that you can overcome this – *you can beat anorexia!* The question is: *Do you want to beat anorexia?* If you aren't certain, read Chapter 2 and then ask yourself this question again. If you know you want to beat anorexia, follow me; Chapter 2 can help cement your desire further, while the chapters thereafter can provide the tools needed to make your desire a reality.

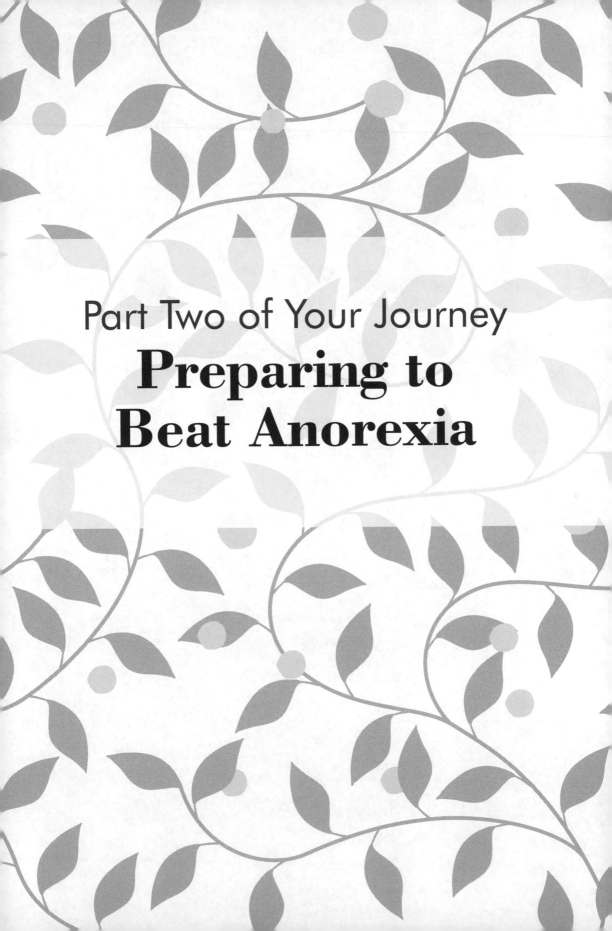

Part Two of Your Journey
# Preparing to Beat Anorexia

Chapter 2

# Why Beat Anorexia?

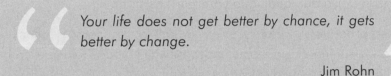

> *Your life does not get better by chance, it gets better by change.*
>
> Jim Rohn

The key reason to beat anorexia is because you deserve to be healthy and happy, but for those with anorexia it can be difficult to recognise this. So, let's take a closer look at the consequences of anorexia and the reasons why you might want to break free from this destructive lifestyle.

## The Physical Consequences of Anorexia

If you are finding it difficult to determine why you should beat anorexia, maybe the severe impact of the condition on both your mind and body could act as some motivation. Indeed, whatever the reasons and pathways of development, anorexia carries with it very serious, sometimes fatal, consequences. These consequences can be gradual and therefore you might not even be aware of just how serious your condition is.

At first, the effects of anorexia, though uncomfortable, do not usually result in serious harm or irreversible damage. Can you relate to any of these short-term consequences of anorexia? Tick all that apply:

- ☐ Weakness

- ☐ Fatigue

- ☐ Dizziness

- ☐ Cold hands and feet

- ☐ Constipation

☐ Bloating

☐ Stomach pains

☐ Dry skin and hair

☐ Headaches

☐ Depression and irritability

☐ Difficulty concentrating and making decisions

☐ Endocrine disorder leading to your periods stopping

As the illness progresses, virtually every organ in the body is affected, resulting in a worsening of symptoms, many of which you wouldn't even be aware of unless you were medically assessed:

- low blood pressure (hypotension)

- slow heartbeat (bradycardia)

- irregular heartbeat (arrhythmia)

- electrolyte imbalances, leading to muscle aches, restlessness, anxiety, headaches, and a whole host of other symptoms

- reduced immune system function, leading to frequent illness

- skin disorders, such as dry or yellow skin, fine hair growth over the body, brittle nails and easy bruising

- stomach ulcers.

While serious, the above conditions can be treated before they lead to irreversible consequences. Without help, however, it becomes more difficult to avoid permanent damage, which can include:

- weakened heart muscle

- osteoporosis

- liver disease

- kidney disease

- infertility.

At the later stages of anorexia, there is a greater risk of death due to heart failure or suicide. Indeed, anorexia is recognised as the leading cause of death of any psychiatric disorder due to this combined effect of physical complications and increased risk of suicide. This fact hasn't been put here to scare you. I know from my own personal experience that very little, not even risk of death, could force me into getting better when I was really ill. However, this information is important for you to know so that you can be equipped to beat this illness when you choose to: so that you have the knowledge to reason with yourself as to why you are embarking on your recovery journey.

# The Psychological and Behavioural Consequences of Anorexia

In addition to the above physical effects, many psychological and behavioural effects result from anorexia. Some of these may have already been present before the onset of the illness and are made worse as it progresses. Take a look at the psychological and behavioural effects listed below and tick any that you are currently experiencing.

- ☐ Clinical depression
- ☐ Low self-esteem
- ☐ Mood swings
- ☐ Withdrawal and social isolation
- ☐ Secretive behaviour with eating and/or exercising
- ☐ Self-harm
- ☐ Substance abuse
- ☐ Aggressiveness when challenged to eat
- ☐ Suicide attempts

The figure below illustrates how anorexia affects your whole mind and body, taking over your very being.

## Anorexia affects your whole body

**Brain and Nerves**
can't think right, fear of gaining weight, sad, moody, irritable, bad memory, fainting, changes in brain chemistry

**Hair**
hair thins and gets brittle

**Heart**
low blood pressure, slow heart rate, fluttering of the heart (palpitations), heart failure

**Blood**
anaemia and other blood problems

**Muscles and Joints**
weak muscles, swollen joints, fractures, osteoporosis

**Kidneys**
kidney stones, kidney failure

**Body Fluids**
low potassium, magnesium and sodium

**Intestines**
constipation, bloating

**Hormones**
periods stop, bone loss, problems growing, trouble getting pregnant; if pregnant higher risk for miscarriage, having a C-section, baby with low birthweight and post-partum depression.

**Skin**
bruise easily, dry skin, growth of fine hair all over body, get cold easily, yellow skin, nails get brittle

Dash line indicates that organ is behind other main organs.

*Source: Office of Women's Health[1]*

# The Gradual Process of Finding Reasons to Overcome Anorexia

It can take a long time for you to recognise that you have a problem and then to find the desire to overcome anorexia. Research shows, however, that the rate of success of anorexia treatment is greater if commenced within three years of development of the illness.[2] So, the sooner you can find that desire and motivation to work towards recovery, the better. Don't despair, however. Recovery *is* possible at any stage. I struggled with eating disorders from my teenage years into my early 30s and I recovered. It is never too late! *If you want to recover, you can recover.*

Initially, you might not recognise or want to overcome the condition. This is due both to the nature of the illness, which has as a hallmark an inability to perceive a correct body image, and also a diminished ability to correctly process thoughts due to the effects that starvation has on the brain. Adding to the complexity of seeking treatment is the fact that because of the anorexia, you might see your behaviours as self-rewarding and positive.

Therefore, that first step towards recovery might take a lot of self-talk and rationalisation – rationalisation that however you currently feel about the anorexia, it is harmful to you now and most certainly harmful to your future.

## Why Do I Want to Beat Anorexia?

So, why might you want to beat anorexia? As highlighted in the previous section, the nature of anorexia might mean the reasons you want to beat the condition come gradually as your mind and body become healthier. What you need now, however, is just one motivating factor to get you started. What is *your* motivating factor? Reasons for recovery might include:

- to understand and address the true root causes of your illness

- to learn to deal with negative emotions such as anger, vulnerability, fear and self-loathing, in a constructive way, without using food

- to explore unhealthy relationships and thought processes that may be contributing to the anorexia

- to restore and maintain physical health

- to ensure a healthy and happy future.

Since anorexia has become a way of coping, you might struggle to reason with yourself as to why you would want to be without it. It is important to acknowledge that anorexia has helped you and to value that. However, there is a better, healthier way to cope with life – a way where you don't have to harm yourself in your efforts to survive.

## Over to You!

✎ So, why beat anorexia? More importantly, why do *you* want to beat anorexia? Take some time out to consider this question and note down some of your thoughts.

_____

_____

_____

_____

_____

Some of you will find this question easier to answer than others, and that is OK. In fact, it is OK to not even know why you might want to beat the illness. It has helped you cope and survive, so it is understandable that you might not feel ready to beat it completely.

✎ With this in mind, let's think about why you might *not* want to beat anorexia (i.e. why you might want to keep anorexia in your life).

_____

_____

_____

_____

_____

Compare your two lists to try to gain some insight into what you can use to motivate yourself to beat anorexia, and what thoughts you need to challenge in order to beat anorexia. For example, maybe you don't want to beat it because it offers you comfort in times of distress. Challenge that thought by finding an alternative form of comfort. Could you curl up on the sofa and watch your favourite film instead? Or spend some time with your pet? There is always an alternative and you have the power to choose that alternative.

| I fear losing anorexia because it helps me... | I could do the following instead, releasing the power anorexia has over me... |
|---|---|
| | |

Whatever your reasons for wanting to beat anorexia, or to hold on to it, seeking the support of others can go a long way in helping you challenge the illness. The next chapter discusses the importance of reaching out to others as you work towards beating anorexia.

# Chapter 3

# **Reaching Out**

> *Sometimes, reaching out and taking someone's hand is the beginning of a journey.*
>
> Vera Nazarian

Living with anorexia can be a lonely place. A heightened fixation on weight and appearance can push you to detach from society and from those who care about you. Indeed, excessive dieting can elicit negative comments from other people, leading to you isolating yourself.[1] This isolation can be convenient when in the grips of anorexia – it allows you to focus on your anorexia-related goals. However, such isolation can hit you hard when you get to a stage where you want to recover and don't have a support network.

Recovering from anorexia requires tremendous amounts of internal strength. However, external support from loved ones, friends and health professionals can help to nurture and maintain that internal strength. So, rather than trying to do this all on your own, be willing to reach out to people you trust. Asking for help is a strength, not a weakness.

## **Different Types of Support**

There are different types of support you can reach out for and you might find you need more of one type than the other (see the table on the next page). You might also find that the type of support you need changes at different stages of your recovery.

| Type of support | Description |
|---|---|
| Information | Knowledge about anorexia and its causes, symptoms and consequences is significant to laying down a foundation for recovery. If you want to beat the condition, you need support in the form of relevant, credible and evidence-based information about anorexia and its available treatments. This will prepare and empower you for the journey ahead and any potential roadblocks. Information can be in the form of written material, expert advice, suggestions and referrals. Information can offer you direction so that you can begin to visualise how to approach recovery. |
| Assistance | Assistance can involve giving or receiving help or material goods. When recovering from anorexia, you can benefit from assistance in carrying out certain daily functions or tasks that you may struggle with as you try to manage your condition. Family members and friends can be the primary source of assistance in this respect, and this support can be as simple as driving you to a medical appointment or going food shopping with you. |
| Belonging (feeling part of something and accepted by others) | Research suggests that anorexia can become a way to cope with lack of self-identify and a low sense of belonging.[2] Many people with anorexia feel that they are cut off from society and find comfort instead in belonging to a 'secret group' whose common purpose is to take control of their eating and physical appearance. You might find you have started to reshape your identity around extreme weight loss and see excessive dieting as a lifestyle rather than an illness. When it comes to recovery, you might find a sense of belonging in group therapy sessions that bring you together with others experiencing the same struggles. Here, you can share stories and personal insights within an atmosphere of mutual understanding. You could also join eating disorder advocacy groups or non-profit organisations that hold events and initiatives to raise awareness and support for anorexia. Group support isn't for everyone, however, and that is OK. Indeed, some people find group support detrimental due to the competitive nature of anorexia. It is important to accurately assess whether group support will benefit or hinder your recovery, as well as to ensure that you still have one-to-one support if you do decide to take the group option. |

| Type of support | Description |
|---|---|
| **Emotional** | Emotional support can take the form of encouragement, understanding, empathy, personal warmth, unconditional love, or sometimes simply by letting a person know you are there if they need you. Recovery from anorexia can be daunting and will require you to confront and address several underlying emotions that may be driving your eating disorder. It is worth learning to be open and accepting of every emotion, whether positive or negative, so that you can better understand how you are using food and weight to deal with deeper emotional issues. Therefore, it is important to have someone who will listen and help you challenge your negative, and at times illogical, perceptions. A great form of emotional support is a counsellor – someone non-judgemental, who you don't feel the need to hold back with. Whether we intend to or not, we might hold back with friends and family through fear of being judged or to protect them from the pain we are experiencing. |
| **Feedback** | In order to monitor whether you are on track with your health goals, feedback can be extremely useful. It can be as simple as someone letting you know when you seem to be diverging from your recovery plan or falling into obsessive behaviours. Feedback from other people is important in monitoring unidentified triggers and keeping your actions and thought processes directed towards recovery. Feedback about your weight, health condition, attitudes and moods, personal relationships and treatment progress will help you to make better health and lifestyle decisions.<br><br>Feedback about emotional and mental progress can come from a counsellor who is helping with your recovery. You might also want a nutritionist to provide feedback on a food diary you are keeping to help you monitor improvements in your diet and your thoughts around food.[3] Feedback from a nutritionist can help with validating and adjusting meal plans and eating behaviours. |

| Relief | Following meal plans and closely watching your actions can be tiring. Consequently, creating a regimented process around food and weight management can be a contributing factor to reverting to anorexia-related behaviours. For this reason, you also need to take a break. You can do this by asking friends and family to interject some spontaneity into your routine by providing fun and pleasurable distractions from the tasks of life.[4] You could also choose to fill some of your days with positive social activities, such as new group activities, volunteering for a special cause, or learning a new hobby. The general goal is to perform rewarding activities with other people where the focus is not on food, weight or anorexia. Instead, the focus is on spending time with others, rebuilding relationships or making new ones, finding a sense of belonging, and infusing enthusiasm and energy back into your life. |
|---|---|

## Over to You!

In this chapter, you have learned about the various types of support and how each can help you beat anorexia. Now, you can better determine what mix of support types you might benefit from.

✎ **What information do you feel you need to help you beat anorexia? Where might you be able to find this information?**

| Information I need | Where could I find this information? |
| --- | --- |
| | |

✎ Name a trusted person or persons who you feel would be willing and able to provide each type of support discussed in this chapter.

| Support type | Who I trust to provide this support |
|---|---|
| Information | |
| Assistance | |
| Belonging | |
| Emotional support | |
| Feedback | |
| Relief | |

Remember that you are a work in progress, and there is no need to beat anorexia alone. When you are ready, start reaching out to other people. A list of organisations that can provide information and support can be found in the appendix.

Chapter 4

# Seeking Professional Support

*The greatest thing in the world is to know how to belong to oneself.*

Michel de Montaigne

The previous chapter explored how reaching out to others can assist with recovery. Reaching out for professional support especially can be an important step towards health. This chapter discusses what counselling is and how you can use it to beat anorexia.

## How Counselling Works

Counselling is a therapeutic or healing relationship between two people in which one, a trained counsellor, helps the other to make positive changes to themselves or their environment.[1] It aims to alleviate distress, resolve personal crises and improve well-being.[2] It can be conducted individually or in groups, face to face or over the phone/Skype, and in a single session or multiple sessions.[3] Essentially, counselling is a conversation between yourself and a trained professional about a mental health issue or problem that you want to overcome – in this case, anorexia.

## The Benefits of Counselling for Anorexia Recovery

Often, anorexia is due to some deep emotional discomfort and so counselling can provide a regular and safe place to explore your most difficult thoughts and feelings. The counsellor is trained to be respectful of any details that you might share, and they will provide support as you try to understand the issues associated with your eating disorder and identify some insights that can be significant to your recovery.

Counselling can help you cope with a stressful situation, explore painful and forgotten issues from the past, deal with negative feelings such as depression and anxiety, break down barriers to anorexia recovery, and gain a better understanding of yourself and greater confidence in your ability to overcome anorexia.

The benefits of counselling are unlikely to be felt immediately because of the complex nature of anorexia, so it is important to commit to the treatment. Indeed, the counselling process may feel like a struggle at the beginning, but over time and with the support of an experienced counsellor, you can start to reap the relief of having someone who acknowledges your deepest thoughts and feelings and helps you to disentangle and take control of them.

## The Different Kinds of Counselling

There are different counselling approaches for treating anorexia, with counsellors using various theoretical orientations to interpret the emotions, thoughts and behaviours of clients. Knowing these different approaches can help you decide which might be best for your specific recovery needs.

The success of any counselling process is highly dependent on your willingness to participate, which in turn is greatly influenced by the counsellor's ability to build rapport and trust. I had a strong and trusting relationship with my counsellor, which developed over several years. The approach we used to address the underlying problems associated with my eating disorder was a mix of psychodynamic, person-centred, cognitive behavioural and inner child work. You might find that you require different approaches at different stages of your journey. For example, I did a lot of deep psychodynamic exploration at the beginning (after building trust with my counsellor) in order to process some of the childhood trauma contributing to my dysfunctional eating. I then moved on to inner child work in order to heal some of this trauma. The more my inner pain was addressed through such techniques, the more able I was to take a cognitive behavioural approach to challenging my thinking and changing my behaviours. Throughout all of these stages, my counsellor was person-centred – genuine, non-judgemental and empathic.

| Type of counselling | How it works | Advantages | Disadvantages |
|---|---|---|---|
| Cognitive behavioural therapy (CBT) | CBT focuses on challenging negative beliefs and patterns of thinking. | It teaches skills that enable you to question unhelpful thinking patterns that might drive the anorexia, including how to react differently to these thoughts.<br><br>It helps you appreciate how a change in behaviour leads to improved mental and emotional states.<br><br>Sessions can include educational elements about nutrition or other areas of need.<br><br>It helps with the obsessive compulsive aspects of anorexia-related behaviour.<br><br>It has clearly defined goals. | Sessions are structured, so you lack flexibility to address what might be bothering you on a particular day.<br><br>It focuses on present problems instead of the past, but anorexia is often rooted to past events or experiences.<br><br>It focuses on practical problem-solving approaches, but anorexia is a very emotional illness. |
| Dialectical behavioural therapy (DBT) | This type of therapy borrows some techniques from CBT, but while CBT focuses on your beliefs, DBT also incorporates your behaviours. It is based on four techniques: mindfulness and how to observe, describe and participate in the moment; distress tolerance by engaging in distraction, self-soothing and consideration of the pros and cons of certain actions; emotional regulation by recognising and identifying barriers to changing negative emotions into positive ones; and interpersonal effectiveness or methods for managing conflicts in relationships. | It is suitable for those who react to negative emotions with extreme and self-harming behaviours, including those with anorexia.<br><br>You will be taught four key skills: increased self-awareness; regulation of self-defeating thoughts; challenging black-and-white thinking; and management of conflict and stress. | It was originally developed for borderline personality disorder and therefore further research is needed on its long-term effectiveness with anorexia recovery. |

| | | | |
|---|---|---|---|
| Interpersonal psychotherapy (IPT) | This therapy focuses on interpersonal issues such as role transitions, unresolved grief or social difficulties. It explores how you relate to others and is grounded on the principle that the state of our mental health affects our social relationships. | It has been found to increase the self-esteem and body image issues of those suffering from eating disorders.[4]<br><br>It provides people with anorexia with skills to identify and express their emotions, skills to recognise how past behaviour and negative thinking have affected the current state of personal relationships, and skills necessary to change the way they think about and respond to social situations.<br><br>It can assist with problematic family relationships, including communication difficulties. | In the long term, because it is focused on improving social relationships, it is not as effective as treatments that take a broader approach to anorexia recovery. |
| Person-centred counselling (PCC) | The main goal of PCC is to facilitate a person's innate ability of reaching their potential to become a fully functional individual. It provides you with a safe non-judgemental place in order to explore your personal growth and self-healing. It also seeks to return you to an awareness of your own unique identity and your own set of values. | You will develop a relationship with your counsellor that provides you with genuine care, understanding and respect.<br><br>It helps improve self-awareness, self-reliance and self-esteem. Since it is directed by the client (you), you get to decide the content and pace of the sessions. | It is non-directive and therefore the counsellor will not steer the conversation: you do, because you are deemed the expert in your own health and well-being. Sometimes people with anorexia do need to be guided, especially when in the denial stage of the illness. |

| Type of counselling | How it works | Advantages | Disadvantages |
|---|---|---|---|
| Psychodynamic therapy | This approach focuses on unravelling some of the unconscious forces that drive your behaviour. It uses techniques such as free association (talking openly about anything and everything without censorship); dream analysis (science-based analysis of dreams and fantasies for information from the unconscious that is too painful to bring to the conscious mind); and transference (directing at the counsellor the negative feelings you have toward another person so that you can bring it out into the open and deal with them). | It is not short-term therapy, which means you will not feel pressure to get well at a particular speed. It may take months or years to explore deeply ingrained thinking patterns and behaviours.<br><br>It takes a historical perspective and examines your personality and early life experiences and how these have influenced your current mental condition, behaviour and relationships. | This therapy is time extensive and often requires years of commitment.<br><br>By taking a historical perspective, much of the focus is on the past rather than how you are now. This can sometimes feel like your symptoms are being ignored. |
| Inner child work | The inner child is that part of the adult personality that houses child-like and adolescent behaviours, memories, emotions and habits. Counsellors help you reconnect with your inner child to enhance your mental health because this therapy presupposes that mental health problems arise when people get disconnected from the child within. This is due to unfulfilled needs in childhood. | It includes a range of approaches that help heal your inner child, including art, music and play.<br><br>It allows you to regain the creativity you had as a child to break the restrictive behaviours of anorexia.<br><br>It allows you to externalise feelings of hurt, vent frustration and express sadness instead of bottling them up inside.<br><br>It teaches the skill of self-soothing, so you can 'mother yourself' and provide yourself with nurturing that will aid you in your recovery. | For those who have experienced particularly traumatic childhoods, such as neglect or sexual abuse, this can take you back to a time when you felt unsafe. It is fundamental that you have a strong relationship with your counsellor before embarking on this type of treatment. |

# Standards for Choosing Counsellors

Most reputable counsellors will have memberships, fellowships or accreditations with major professional associations, such as the British Association for Counselling and Psychotherapy (BACP), the National Counselling Society, the British Association for Behavioural and Cognitive Psychotherapies (BABCP) and the British Psychological Society (BPS).

Some of the questions to ask a potential counsellor are:

- Are you licensed/accredited?

- What are your academic qualifications and training credentials?

- What is the theoretical orientation of your practice?

- What are your qualifications within this orientation?

- Do you work strictly within this orientation or can we be flexible?

- How do you adhere to ethical principles around confidentiality and setting boundaries? Most counsellors maintain confidentiality unless you are at risk of harm to yourself or others, and this is ultimately because your safety matters (even if you don't feel worthy of care or concern).

- What do I do if I am unhappy with our work together?

- Have you previously worked with clients who have anorexia?

Add to this list if you can think of any other questions you would like to ask a potential counsellor. You are in complete control of who you choose to work with.

Despite having the credentials and experience, being at ease and feeling that you are opening yourself up to a trustworthy person in a safe environment is key to successful counselling. After selecting a counsellor to work with, it is important to assess how the relationship progresses and to ask yourself:[5]

- Do I feel that the counsellor is listening to me without judgement?

- Do I trust this counsellor with my emotions, thoughts and problems?

- Do I feel like my counsellor is doing their best to make the most out of every session?

- Can I see myself recovering with the support of this counsellor?

## Over to You!

In this section, you have gained a better understanding of what counselling is, how it works, what the benefits are, and how it can facilitate recovery from anorexia. Complete the following exercises to explore how you can incorporate counselling into your personal recovery plan.

✎ **Review your personal health goals. How can you upgrade these goals with the assistance of a trained counsellor?**

_____

_____

_____

_____

_____

✎ **Thinking about the types of counselling approaches discussed in this chapter, make a list of what you believe are the pros and cons of each type. Reflect on your list to determine which type might be most appropriate to your own recovery needs.**

| Approach | Pros | Cons |
|---|---|---|
| Cognitive behavioural therapy | | |
| Dialectic behavioural therapy | | |

| | | |
|---|---|---|
| Interpersonal psychotherapy | | |
| Person-centred counselling | | |
| Psychodynamic therapy | | |
| Inner child work | | |
| Which approach suits you the best and why? | | |

It is important to note that when seeking help from your GP, not all of these types of therapy are available. CBT tends to be the most popular, but understanding the other types of therapies and the benefits that each approach offers may allow you to communicate your specific needs to your counsellor. Ultimately, all types of therapy can help if you have the right counsellor, so even if you don't get access to the approach you feel will benefit you the most, still give it your all – all support matters.

Beating anorexia requires strong commitment on your part, but having a supportive professional counsellor at your side can go a long way in helping you on your journey to beat anorexia. Now let's take a look at your next step in that journey.

Chapter 5

# Beating Anorexia
# from All Angles

> *The courage to live brings its own rewards.*
>
> Rachel Schade

When we speak of beating anorexia, it's common for people to assume that we are simply referring to gaining weight. For cases of severe malnourishment where the life of a person is already at risk, doctors will make weight gain a priority. However, you don't have to wait until you get to this point; you can take control yourself – now. Furthermore, in this chapter you will learn that weight is only part of the problem. You might even discover that your condition has nothing to do with weight, but that weight is simply your way of coping with other problems. Ultimately, recovery is about *you*, your *health*, your *happiness* and your overall well-being – and in order to achieve these, you need to come at your illness from many different angles. You need to be *willing*, *ready* and *confident*.

## What Does It Take to Beat Anorexia?

So, what is beating anorexia truly about? It requires embracing a lifestyle change – one that begins with the mind. It isn't just about changing what you eat or what you do, but *wanting* to make changes to how you live the rest of your life. To jumpstart your beating anorexia journey, you need to begin by looking closely at your attitudes and behaviours. From there, you need to develop the *willingness*, *readiness* and *confidence* to make the changes required to beat your illness.

## Be Willing

Do you really want to live a healthier life? If yes, then you need to be *willing* to look at various aspects of your life, such as the habits and routines that are contributing towards the anorexia. Next, you need to be *willing* to take steps towards reducing or getting rid of these destructive habits.

Rather than focusing on your physical weight, start considering your mental weight and cutting down on the excess weight in your mind – the unhealthy attitudes and habits that are maintaining the anorexia. Some examples of mental weight include the following:

- **Giving in to deeply ingrained unhealthy eating rituals:** 'I must eat the same foods at the same time each day.'

- **Fearing what others might say about your attempts at making a serious change:** 'People see me as someone who is in control of her food. What will they think of me if I start eating more?'

- **Postponing lifestyle change plans and blaming it on work demands, peer pressure or family issues:** 'I want to get better, but I need to wait until I am out of this stressful job.'

If you aren't willing to examine and identify your unhealthy mental patterns and attitudes, you may find it difficult to motivate yourself to accept and maintain change. In which case, any changes you make will only yield short-term results.

## Be Ready

Health psychologists use something known as the Readiness to Change scale to help people change unhealthy behaviours, including behaviours related to anorexia. Understanding and using this tool yourself can help you progress through your journey to beat anorexia. In particular, if you have been unsuccessful in changing your lifestyle in the past, this tool can help you evaluate the obstacles that may be in your way.

The Readiness to Change scale involves six main stages, as presented below. Which one do you think you are in when it comes to being ready to beat anorexia?

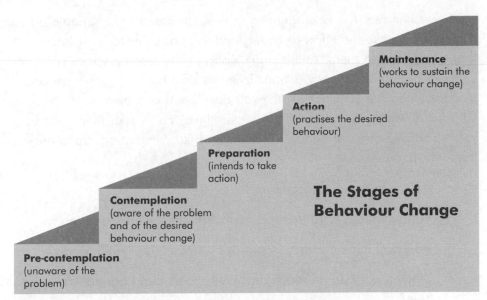

Source: Prochaska, DiClemente and Norcross[2]

## Stage 1: Pre-Contemplation

If you are in the pre-contemplation stage, you aren't yet ready to take action to beat your anorexia. You don't recognise the problem (in this case, anorexia), even though everyone around you can. Being stuck in this stage leads to resistance to change and small setbacks can be demoralising enough to give up on any preparation for change. To move past this stage, you need to listen to those around you and trust that they aren't concerned about you for no reason. Rather than ignoring them, be open to exploring the fact that they might be right. You have nothing to lose from giving them the benefit of the doubt, except from an illness that could be potentially fatal.

## Stage 2: Contemplation

By recognising the problem and seeking solutions, you have moved into the contemplation stage. In this case, the problem is anorexia and the solution is to change your lifestyle and the way you cope with the thoughts, emotions and the events of life. If you are in this stage, you want to start on the road to change and have realised that, with active effort, you can start to move towards your goal of beating anorexia. However, you are still struggling; you want to change your lifestyle, but you can't clearly see the specific obstacles in your way in order to reach your end goal.

There is a real risk of stagnating in this stage and many people do so if they don't make the effort to understand the obstacles to lifestyle change that are specific to them. At this stage, you may be making vague plans for change, but not taking any action. To move past this stage, it is important to understand the specifics of why you developed anorexia. Refer back to Chapter 1 where you explored the factors involved in your illness. To help you gain further insight and to move beyond Contemplation, try to answer the following questions:

- How is anorexia affecting my life?

- What makes it hard to implement changes towards recovery?

- How do I think my life will improve if I reach my health goals?

- What could I do if I reach my health goals that I am not able to do now?

## Stage 3: Preparation

At this stage, you are planning to make changes imminently. Preparation is very important to the success of your goals and there are several steps that can be taken at this point to increase your chances of moving steadily through the stages of change.

First, it is important to make your goals public to those you trust to be supportive. Making your goals public within your support network will allow you to draw on their help and guidance when you are under stress. Including trusted family and friends in your plans can also help lessen any hesitancy you may be feeling and will help motivate you to move forward.

When you do choose to move forward, preparation is key. People who don't plan properly often find they are unable to overcome any challenges they face in the next stage of change – Action.

## Stage 4: Action

Once you have a plan, you can move into the action stage of lifestyle change. This is when you start to make your goals real. You need to enter this stage with a clear picture of what is required on a day-to-day basis and how you are going to deal with challenges. Remember that there will be setbacks along the way and it is important to have a plan for how to deal with them effectively, so that they don't trip you up completely.

This stage will require commitment in both energy and time. The Action stage is when you will start to notice improvements. Keep track of your achievements and throughout this stage ask yourself the following questions in order to reinforce the positive effects of your efforts:

- What positive changes have I noticed Io my health and well-being?

- How have the changes I have made affected the way I feel about myself?

- Do I have the energy to do more now?

- How do I picture myself six months from now if I continue this journey?

- How will family and friends react when I reach my goal?

## Stage 5: Maintenance

Although action may feel like the hardest and most important part of the Readiness to Change stages, maintenance is just as important. However, don't panic. You aren't at this stage yet, and by the time you reach this stage, you will have developed many tools to help you maintain your new-found health and it will seem less scary for you. At the moment, it might seem an impossible place to reach, but you can reach it and this book has been designed to help you get there.

Stage 5 (Maintenance) of your journey can be removed from your mind for now; we will revisit it in Chapter 11, when we explore relapse prevention strategies.

It is likely that you are in the Preparation stage of recovery, hence why you are reading this book. So, let's start building your confidence to make it to the Action stage.

## Be Confident

Readiness and willingness can get one foot in the door and be catalysts for developing a healthy lifestyle. Sticking to a plan and getting the other foot moving, however, requires *confidence*. How certain are you that you can move from thinking about change towards applying what you learn in this book and actually making changes?

Beating anorexia requires that you are confident in your ability to handle the physical, psychological and social demands of the journey you are embarking on. In particular, there are four factors that shape confidence and can be used to improve success at beating anorexia: mastery experiences, vicarious experiences, verbal persuasion and physiological states.

## Mastery Experiences

Mastery experiences are when you are successful at adopting a behaviour you believe is difficult, such as eating three meals a day. Past successful experiences of mastery are thought to be the key to creating high levels of confidence.[3] Success builds confidence in your ability to implement change in your life, while not succeeding undermines that confidence. In some cases, it may not be lack of succe ss that hinders self-confidence. Someone struggling with anorexia is not familiar with the sense of mastery due to their ongoing obsession with weight and perceived failure. Even if competent in other areas of their life, this sense of failure, related to the eating disorder, can colour all areas of their life and create a sense of incompetence.

Achieving mastery of a particular behaviour, such as eating a nutritious diet or restricting exercise, is no small feat and should be approached through setting realistic, attainable goals; goals that are too ambitious can lead to a sense of failure and diminished confidence. Changing anorexia-related behaviours needs to be taken in small steps. Starting with short-term goals is crucial to accomplishing a sense of mastery. This may mean you need to set goals for 60-minute periods, giving you a sense of control over the goal and being able to realistically achieve it. It is likely that you are someone who aims high with your goals and you might need to adjust the way you think about goal setting – small goals are just as important as large goals. Indeed, it is the achievement of small goals that helps us get closer to reaching our larger, more ambitious goals.

## Vicarious Experiences

Vicarious experiences are those felt through the observation of another person's actions. Observing other people achieve success in tackling recovery from anorexia can allow you to see your capacity for similar forms of success. For vicarious experience to be helpful in addressing personal struggles, the person whose behaviour is being modelled must not only be seen as having achieved success after attempting something difficult, but they must also have similar characteristics such as age, class, gender, personal history and present challenges. The greater the similarity, the greater the impact their success will have on someone recovering from anorexia. If you can't relate to the person or the circumstances, it is harder to think, 'If they can do it, then so can I.'

You do need to be careful how you are modelling others; don't set yourself up for the unachievable. Ideally, a model will be a peer or social equal. Furthermore, the goal of modelling needs to be improvement of self, rather than trying to be like someone else. The important lesson is building confidence, learning determination and persevering when faced with obstacles.

*A word of caution:* It is possible that watching someone else succeed at something you are trying so hard to achieve can work against your confidence to accomplish the same. If you find that it is reinforcing feelings of incompetency, you may need to change your role model.[4]

## Verbal Persuasion

Verbal persuasion refers to positive encouragement that boosts a sense of capacity to initiate and sustain change, especially when encountering obstacles. When seeking sources of verbal persuasion, it is important to find people with similar experiences, such as others who have struggled with anorexia and/or changing their lifestyle. When verbal persuasion succeeds in enabling a person to meet their lifestyle goals through hard times, this builds mastery.

When it comes to anorexia recovery, verbal persuasion from others is not as important as self-persuasion. So not being self-critical is just as important as giving yourself praise. Your voice, beliefs and thoughts are potent tools that underpin your sense of self-worth. It may seem overly simplified, but there is strong therapeutic value in using positive self-affirmations. In place of the mantras you know so well (such as 'I look terrible' or 'I hate my body'), challenge those words with positive affirmations (such as 'I respect my body' or 'I am accepting myself more each day').[5] Use of the tool of positive self-talk, when combined with mastery experiences, makes for a dynamic combination for enhancing your confidence.

## Physiological States

Physiological and emotional states directly affect confidence, but the impact can be greater in those who spend much of their time fighting physiological states such as hunger or fullness, or feelings of sadness and anger. For those with anorexia, most physiological states are associated with a lowering of confidence, with the exception of hunger – this becomes a sign of success, of being in control. This needs to be challenged and you can start by finding other physiological states that make you feel good about yourself – at least until you are far enough into your recovery to view hunger as a negative rather than a positive. Positive physiological states include feeling rested or relaxed, excited, warm and cosy, or in love. Can you think of any others?

Working on raising your confidence is only one part of overcoming anorexia, but it is one of the most important parts – it puts your sense of control in the foreground, challenging you to seek solutions and maintain successes. Seeing improvement in how you think and behave, and especially in your capacity to direct your own change, is a more meaningful indicator of success than simply measuring weight loss by the pound.

## Over to You!

This chapter has explained how beating anorexia goes beyond food and weight. It is also mainly about a deep mental shift that requires you to be *ready*, *willing* and *confident* to make a genuine change to your overall lifestyle and, ultimately, to be kind to yourself. Take some time to reflect on the following questions.

✎ **What makes up my 'mental weight'? How do these habits, attitudes and behaviours contribute towards anorexia?**

_____

_____

_____

_____

_____

✎ How ready am I to beat anorexia? (Use the readiness ruler below to measure your level of readiness on a scale of 0 to 10, with 10 being the most ready.)

My level of readiness:

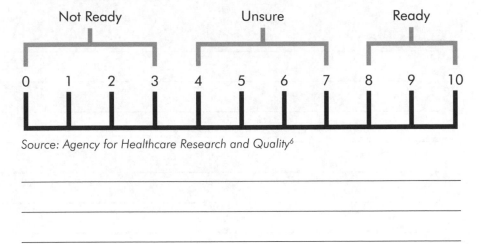

Source: Agency for Healthcare Research and Quality[6]

_____

_____

_____

_____

_____

✎ Am I willing and motivated to commit to the necessary changes to beat anorexia? (Use the scales below to measure your level of willingness and motivation on a scale of 0 to 10, with 10 being the most willing or motivated.)

My level of willingness:

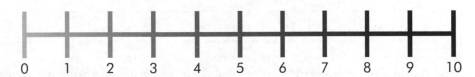

## My level of motivation:

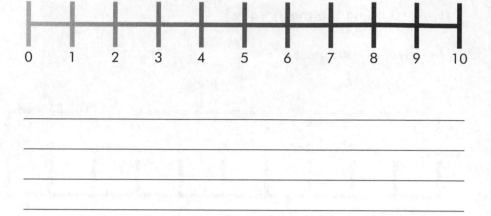

_____

_____

_____

_____

_____

_____

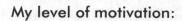 **Do I believe that I can beat anorexia? What will it take psychologically, behaviourally, physically and socially to beat anorexia?**

_____

_____

_____

_____

_____

_____

You might find you need to work on your willingness, motivation and confidence before you move to Part 3 of your journey – beating anorexia by taking control. If this is the case, think about what might increase your ratings on these scales. For example, maybe you can increase your willingness by deciding to be more open-minded to the possibility that you are ill. Thinking back to the negative impact of anorexia on your health could be one way to increase your motivation, and looking to a previously difficult achievement might increase your confidence. Factors that will increase your ratings in these important areas of recovery are unique to everyone, so what are yours? Maybe even 'dipping' into the next stage of your journey and learning some of the coping tools discussed in the next chapters might assist? When you are ready, Part 3 of your journey is awaiting you with open arms.

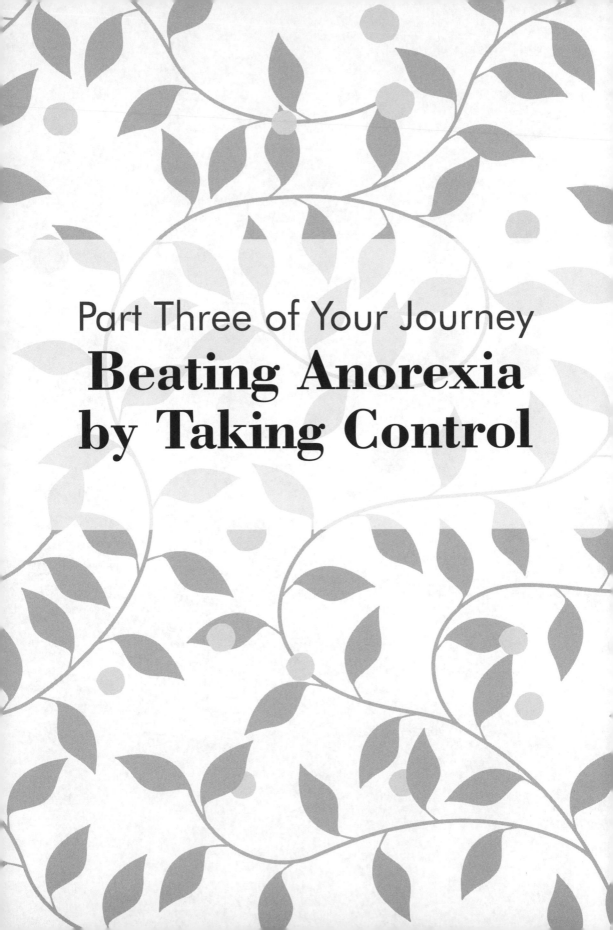

Part Three of Your Journey
# Beating Anorexia by Taking Control

Chapter 6

# Taking Control of Your Behaviour

> *If you take control of your behaviour, your emotions will fall into place.*
>
> John C. Maxwell

Developing a healthy relationship with food is a necessary aspect of long-term recovery from anorexia. While doing so may seem overwhelming if you have engaged in disordered eating for a long time, taking small, deliberate steps can bring about positive and gradual change in terms of your behaviour around food. This chapter provides some guidance on taking control of your behaviour in a way that will help you towards your recovery.

## Create a Self-Soothing Toolkit to Support Healthy Eating

Re-establishing a regular eating routine can be an emotionally challenging experience. Therefore, it is important to accompany a new meal plan with tools to address the uncomfortable feelings and thoughts that can surface when new eating habits are introduced. Of particular importance are self-soothing tools and techniques. In fact, the ability to self-soothe is one of the most essential tools a person can use when it comes to anorexia recovery.[1] Disordered eating can be an attempt to self-soothe, so ceasing unhealthy eating behaviour may increase the need for emotional comfort. Replacing restrictive eating and fasting with healthy coping skills is, therefore, a necessary component of a healthy meal plan. So don't leave yourself emotionally vulnerable when you are most likely to be triggered: create a self-soothing toolkit *before* you launch into a new eating plan.

Self-soothing tools can include:

- a recovery journal

- meditation tapes or audios

- music

- relaxing rituals such as short walks after meals, yoga or stretching routines upon rising and before bed

- breathing exercises

- art or colouring in

- talking with a designated 'recovery buddy' or support person

- anything else that will help you experience and manage emotions in ways other than harming yourself through anorexia-related thoughts and behaviours.

Such tools are helpful for processing negative emotions such as anxiety and fear, as well as for distracting from obsessive thinking around food and weight, which may persist for some time after normal eating patterns are established.

*Remember:* The key to any new tool being effective – including self-soothing tools – is practice, patience and curiosity. Be open to trying new ways of dealing with discomfort, and always keep in mind that change takes time. As your body and brain begin to heal, your feelings and attitudes will change for the better.

## Keep a Food Diary

A multi-purpose food diary is another great tool for supporting both the behavioural and emotional aspects of a new healthy eating routine. Use your diary to record your meal plan and goals, such as increasing portion size, introducing previously 'forbidden' foods and eating in restaurants. Along with planning and scheduling meals in your diary, you might find it useful to write about how you feel before and after eating. Jotting down such thoughts can get them out of your head and provide objective distance and a chance for you to rationalise any unhelpful thoughts. When you see in writing what goes on in your mind, you can begin to better understand your irrational or fear-based thinking and to address it with practical strategies. You may want to share your diary with a nutritionist, counsellor or friend, and use it as a way to mark progress, map intentions for the future and troubleshoot if you've faced a setback.

You might want to start working with the diary template below, but do change the columns to suit your own needs so that you can gain the information you feel will help you the most in your recovery.

## Food Diary
Day/Date

| When & where? Time & location | What I ate & drank | Do I feel I ate too much? | V/L/D | Exercise: what and how long? | Comments (Write down any thoughts, feelings, triggers, important events or circumstances, weight, etc.) |
|---|---|---|---|---|---|
| | | | | | |

Carry the food diary with you at all times and write as soon as possible after eating/drinking.
Record all eating and drinking, with simple descriptions of quantities. Do not weigh food or count calories.
V = vomit, L = laxatives, D = diuretics (and how many if taken)

Source: Getselfhelp[2]

Be totally honest when completing your food diary – be honest with yourself and with whoever you might share it with. This can be difficult due to the secretive nature of anorexia and the sense of shame that can come from eating. However, be brave – it is only through honesty that you will be able to better understand the driving forces behind anorexia-related behaviours and how to overcome those forces.

## Adaptive Eating: Finding Balance and a Routine That Works for You

Given the contradictory and often extreme messages about food in the media, establishing a normal routine can be challenging for anyone, especially those with a history of anorexia. However, finding a balanced and intuitive way to feed yourself after long periods of disordered eating *is* possible. With patience and self-compassion, as well as a sound nutrition plan, the body and mind will eventually regain a sense of balance and well-being.

In order to develop a healthy eating routine that you are also able to enjoy, you might find these steps useful:

⇨ Make a list of various foods or food groups and rate them in terms of how difficult they are to reintroduce into your diet; start with the easiest.

⇨ Talk to a nutritionist and develop an eating plan that you are comfortable with.

⇨ Cook for yourself as often as possible (the preparation process can be as enjoyable as the meal).

⇨ Take your time with meals; don't rush them or try to get them over with.

⇨ If you are required to eat out, try to focus less on food and more on new experiences.

⇨ Be grateful for the food you are eating – it is giving you the energy to enjoy life and to recover.

⇨ See food as the necessity that it is – just like a car can't function without fuel, you can't function efficiently without the energy from food.

⇨ Develop an interest in how the nutrients in certain foods are nurturing your mind or body. For example, if you have a chicken sandwich, the bread is supplying you with fibre and the chicken with protein. Even a scraping of butter provides you with vitamin A. Take this even further. The fibre is improving your digestion, the protein is keeping the cells in your body healthy (your hair and nails are mostly made up of protein), and the vitamin A helps fight infection.

Drinking water is another important component of your nutritional routine. Every system in your body needs water for it to function properly. When I was at my worst, I even found drinking water difficult due to the sense of fullness that comes from it. I would take miniscule sips throughout the day and needed prompting to ensure I stayed hydrated. You need water to live and it will also positively influence how you feel mentally and physically. It will also help you to better evaluate your hunger and fullness levels, which can be difficult at the beginning of recovery.

## What Is Healthy Eating?

Normal or healthy eating (also known as 'intuitive eating' or 'mindful eating') involves feeding the body what it needs to perform daily activities and endure occasional stress. Specifically, it consists of rejecting the dieting mentality, eating when hungry, stopping when satisfied, and every now and again indulging in treats or cravings without labelling foods 'forbidden' or compensating with purging behaviour. Intuitive eating is about satisfying physical hunger as opposed to emotional needs, although it also means eating in a way that brings pleasure and satisfaction on a sensory and emotional level.

In the earliest stages of recovery from anorexia, intuitive eating may be unrealistic; it is likely to take some time to build a sense of trust in your body and regain your appetite, both of which are key components of intuitive eating. For those who have shut down their sense of hunger and satiety, structured meal plans may work better to support recovery and stimulate the appetite. However, as the recovery process unfolds and the body begins to heal, integrating intuitive eating for certain meals or days of the week is one approach you can take. Always do what feels best for *you*! There is no right or wrong way when it comes to reintroducing a healthier way of eating.

Beginning to normalise eating is best done with the support of a nutritionist if possible, especially at the beginning of your recovery where you might have lost sight of what a nutritious diet looks like. Following guidelines for eating balanced and nourishing meals that provide adequate energy requirements will ensure your nutritional needs are being met while reducing anxiety about weight gain.

Notice any feelings that arise around your new eating plan, and jot them down in your diary. Dealing with any resistance to eating is part of recovery. While it is important to adopt an open mind regarding food choices and to avoid restricting, it is also OK to approach previously forbidden foods slowly and to make changes gradually.

Here are some general approaches you might want to consider when changing your behaviour around food:

⇨ Start by feeding yourself small balanced meals three times a day and two to three snacks as needed. Eating small portions every two to three hours may be the best way to accommodate your body's needs and give the body time to adjust to regular meals.

⇨ Because blood sugar is lowest in the morning and the stress hormone cortisol is at its highest, starting each day with a balanced breakfast will help keep your energy levels and mood balanced, which will ultimately help you remain focused on your recovery journey.

⇨ Start with small to normal portions of healthy foods and gradually build up to larger portions.

⇨ Keep in mind that you may experience early feelings of fullness as you reintroduce normal-sized portions. The best way to deal with the physical and psychological discomfort this may cause is distraction. If you find yourself obsessing about how much you ate or find that your anxiety levels increase after meals when you are 'too full', try to keep busy doing something you love, something you are good at or something that will take your attention off your body as your digestion stabilises. As you eat more regular meals, early fullness should subside. Until then, self-soothe and move your attention away from your body. If you find these times particularly difficult, it might be useful to ensure that you have someone with you after meals to keep you occupied and prevent you from purging.

⇨ Be gentle with yourself and practise self-compassion. Recovery takes time.

## Getting to Grips with Hunger and Fullness

One of my biggest challenges to recovery was learning how to recognise feelings of hunger and fullness. With anorexia, these physiological feelings can become so entwined with emotions that we can't accurately recognise them. Then, because we deny our body food when it is hungry or punish it when we feel full, we stop being able to interpret what our body is trying to tell us. This can be made even more difficult by the fact that, initially, you will feel 'full' on only small amounts of food because your body may have become used to starvation mode. There is also a lack of trust in our body and a fear that we won't know when to stop or when we have eaten too much. I had to take a step back and literally teach myself as you might a newborn baby how to interpret my body. I had to accept that identifying hunger and fullness was simply something I couldn't do and would have to learn. The good news is that the body is naturally programmed to recognise and respond to hunger and fullness when we allow it to do so and don't bombard it with anorexia-related thoughts and behaviours. It takes time, but it can be done, and the hunger scale below can be a good starting point.

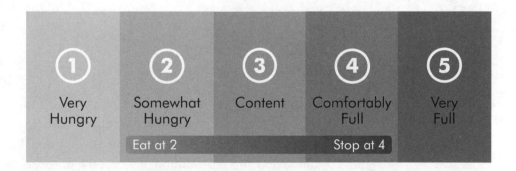

This scale can also help you identify when to eat and when to stop eating – something that can feel quite daunting at the outset of recovery. It can be dangerous to eat when in the 'very hungry' range as this is a recipe for anorexia-related thoughts and feelings, so always try to eat when you are 'somewhat hungry' and before you become ravenous. Extreme hunger can make you feel out of control and scared of eating too much. If you eat when you are at level 2 on the hunger scale, you can remain in control of your food intake and start to associate eating (rather than not eating) as being totally within your control. If you find it really difficult to work with hunger, remember that the body usually needs to refuel every three to four hours. This can be a useful marker as you initially learn to recognise and trust your body's signals.

# Weighing and Other Ritualistic Behaviours

Full recovery from anorexia is about more than letting go of restrictive eating. You will also need to let go of any ritualistic behaviours that support the anorexia. Ritualistic behaviour can include the following (tick any that you are currently experiencing):

☐ Weighing yourself multiple times daily

☐ Body-checking

☐ Cutting food into tiny pieces

☐ Weighing and measuring food

☐ Using the same cutlery or bowls for every meal

☐ Eating in the same place

☐ Eating at the same time

☐ Reading recipe books while hungry

☐ Cooking for others, but not allowing yourself any

Obsessive behaviour can cause you to feel a false sense of control and safety; often, people turn to obsession to cope with negative feelings, emotions and circumstances that are perceived as overwhelming. Although obsession is usually quite draining and time-consuming, it serves the purpose of helping you feel temporarily secure, even if the means are ultimately destructive and the relief is short-lived.

As scary as it can be to think about letting go of behaviours that offer you this short-term relief, you will eventually find that the sense of control you sought through controlling certain actions around food is actually best achieved by letting destructive habits go. This is because obsessive compulsive activities tend to sustain anxiety in the long term since they prevent you from addressing underlying issues.

My obsession was weighing and numbers. I would weigh myself several times a day – when I woke up, before bed, after meals and after a purging episode. It wasn't until I threw my scales away that I could truly focus on recovery. I had convinced myself that I could recover and still weigh myself this often, but that was me not being able to quite let go of the eating disorder. It was impossible to work towards getting better while I was trying to avoid certain numbers on the scales. It took me years to finally be able to free myself of the scales; it was a terrifying concept – to not know how much I weighed and whether I had taken recovery 'too far' and become unhealthily overweight. However, this was the fear-inducing words of the anorexia, not the part of me that wanted to recover.

Whatever your obsession is, whenever you feel it coming on, ask yourself what you are feeling emotionally and what self-soothing strategy you could use to help with that emotion.

## Resisting Purging Behaviours and Learning to Stay with Yourself

Vomiting, laxative abuse, use of slimming pills and fasting are compensatory behaviours commonly used to purge or 'make up for' food intake that feels unsafe or 'excessive'. Any recovery programme must address and seek to eradicate such behaviours as well as find out why these self-harming behaviours are being used. Most of all, you will need to learn to gently resist the 'urge to purge' and tolerate the feelings and thoughts that arise without acting on them. Adopting an attitude of curiosity and openness regarding any emotions that may surface will help you find ways to truly care for yourself. Importantly, like other cravings, the desire to purge will eventually pass, as you begin to feel comfortable tolerating your feelings and develop a new way of relating to them. Finding safe alternatives to purging is, however, critical, as purging behaviours are dangerous and can even be fatal.

Perhaps the most efficient way to reduce the desire to purge is learning to stay with yourself in the face of uncomfortable emotions. Often, those who suffer from eating disorders become so reliant on using purging as a coping strategy that doing so seems automatic. However, purging is cyclical; this means it happens as part of a cycle and that it is a response to something that occurs (such as eating or feeling full). Breaking down this cycle and understanding it is a critical first step. Once you understand how and why you use purging, you can begin to disrupt the cycle with some of the following actions:

⇨ **Develop a '15-minute rule'.** Distract yourself for 15 minutes and then see if the urge is still there. If it isn't, commend yourself for resisting the urge. If the urge is still there, can you extend it for another 15 minutes? Setting yourself goals like this puts you back in control and helps you see that you have a choice about whether you listen to that urge.

⇨ **Use visualisation.** What does the urge to purge look like? A wave that you can surf your way through? A storm you can shelter yourself from? Visualise the urge and what you will do to disempower it.

⇨ **Acknowledge your achievements.** Write a list of the achievements you have made so far on your recovery journey. Read that list out loud and bask in the pride you deserve to feel.

⇨ **Keep a jar of motivation.** Have a jar that you can fill with small pieces of paper with individual reasons why you want to recover or don't want to purge written on them. Turn to this jar whenever you feel you need extra motivation.

⇨ **Express yourself.** Write about or draw how you are feeling; release your emotions in healthier ways.

⇨ **Turn to your distraction list.** Keep a list of distractions that you can turn to during times when you might not be thinking straight.

⇨ **Do the opposite.** Rather than harm yourself, nurture yourself – have a bubble bath, moisturise your skin, ask a loved one for a hug.

Learning how to resist the urge to purge will include some trial and error, so don't beat yourself up if something doesn't work. The important thing is to try new strategies and to build up your own toolkit of ones that work.

## Stopping Obsessive and Excessive Exercise

Many people with anorexia use exercise as a method to purge calories. Compulsive exercise is an unhealthy coping effort that seeks to provide comfort and a sense of control over your life. While exercise is a healthy part of life, overdoing it can damage the body and contribute to a lifestyle that supports anorexia. If you exercise compulsively and do so as a method of purging, ceasing this behaviour is integral to your recovery.

Moderate exercise is healthy for medically stable individuals, and according to the UK Department of Health, adults are recommended to spend at least 150 minutes per week doing moderate activity or 75 minutes per week of vigorous activity.[3] Examples of moderate activity includes brisk walking, swimming laps and heavy gardening or housework. Vigorous activity includes tennis, hiking and running. Those who use exercise to cope with anxiety or to purge could easily do this amount of activity in a single day.

The chances are that if you exercise more than anyone you know, work out when you are sick, injured or exhausted, or do so to punish yourself or compensate for eating, you have a problem with compulsive exercise. If your mood changes radically when you miss a workout, or you find yourself compromising time with family, friends or work to perform workouts, the role exercise plays in your life is unhealthy. Other signs of an unhealthy relationship with exercise include depriving yourself of food or becoming panicked or irritable when you can't exercise.

Giving up compulsive exercise is as anxiety-provoking as abstaining from any other addictive substance, so you will want to make sure you replace the exercise with an activity you find soothing and comforting. Integrating daily meditation into your routine can provide relief from anxiety related to a major lifestyle change and help reduce stress overall. Eventually, finding a balanced way to exercise that will support health without taxing the body or contributing to addictive behaviour is possible. This is something we will explore in more depth in Chapter 7, when we discuss physical well-being.

Now let's delve a bit deeper into how you can take control of the various aspects of your behaviour discussed within this chapter.

## Over to You!

✎ Make a list of activities that comfort you. What are your favourite self-soothing techniques? Consider ways you've comforted yourself in the past.

_____

_____

_____

_____

_____

_____

_____

Keep a record of the list you create and place a copy somewhere you can access it whenever you need it. Practise using the tools when you are not in a state of acute distress. It will be easier to turn to these tools if you have some experience using them. Your brain will eventually create pathways around whatever behaviours you practise, so the more you use these tools, the easier it will be to soothe yourself when you are emotionally triggered.

✎ Write down the strategies you will use if the urge to restrict or skip meals arises.

_____

_____

_____

_____

_____

_____

✎ What are the ritualistic behaviours you engage in? Make a list. Then come up with ways to address each one using a self-soothing tool or replacing the behaviour altogether with a new, fun activity.

| Ritualistic behaviour | New behaviour | Self-soothing tool |
|---|---|---|
| | | |
| | | |
| | | |
| | | |
| | | |
| | | |
| | | |

Once you have tried replacing ritualistic behaviours with new behaviours or self-soothing, take some time to think about how the experience was. How did it feel? Was it helpful? Rate its effectiveness on a scale of 1–10, with 10 being most effective. If it fell beneath a 6 or 7 on the scale, you might want to eliminate it from the toolbox or, alternatively, continue to practise the new behaviour or self-soothing tool in order to hone it. Use this scale to select the tools that are most effective. Rather than obsess about numbers in an unhealthy way, use your perfectionistic nature to analyse numbers that will help you! Recovery doesn't mean you have to lose all of the traits that might be contributing to anorexia – instead, redirect those traits. You have the power to do that; you just need to work on believing that you deserve to do that.

✎ **What purging behaviours do you engage in? Consider a recent purging episode and what caused it. Who or what was involved and what feelings triggered it?**

_____

_____

_____

_____

_____

_____

_____

✎ Make a list of anything you do to compensate for eating. What purpose does the purging serve? Consider the emotional impact and feelings the behaviour brings about. What are some other ways you can support yourself?

| Purging behaviour | Purpose | Emotional impact | What could I do instead? |
|---|---|---|---|
|  |  |  |  |

With more control over your behaviour, you will be better equipped to take control of your physical well-being, which is the topic of the next chapter.

## Chapter 7

# Taking Control of Your Physical Well-Being

> "" *Take care of your body. It's the only place you have to live.*
>
> Jim Rohn ""

Depriving the body of food for long periods of time damages many organs in the body and impairs several bodily systems. With anorexia, people may lose the ability to recognise the body's natural cues such as hunger and pain. To improve your physical well-being, you will need to evaluate and adjust your perspective on hunger, exercise and weight. This may be one of the most challenging parts on your road to recovery, but with time, patience and self-compassion you can learn to fulfil your body's need for food and physical activity. In fact, the two go hand in hand; food fuels physical activity and physical activity uses the energy from food. There is an ongoing cycle between food (energy in) and physical activity (energy out).

## Acknowledge and Respect Hunger and Fullness Cues

People with anorexia often experience feelings of anxiety or guilt when they need to respond to hunger. Embarking on the road to recovery entails learning how to respect and listen to your body. Hunger is the body's way of telling you that it needs food. In this respect, hunger is your friend – not your enemy. It is telling you exactly what you need to meet your energy requirements.

Saying, 'No thank you, I'm not hungry,' when someone offers you food might have become a habit. Try to avoid making this automatic response. If you continue to ignore your body's needs, any effort towards recovery can become fruitless. Without the right amount of energy, you will find it difficult to rebuild your organs and muscles and summon the strength to manage the anxieties that may come your way.

You also need to be mindful of the feeling of fullness. Eating a little and convincing yourself that you are full is something you need to watch out for. Once you start eating more, your body will experience hunger more frequently. And if hunger always comes soon after you eat, or you feel dizzy and irritable even after eating, then these may indicate that you did not eat enough.[1] Eventually, as your body recovers, fullness should feel like you have eaten an adequate amount without feeling any type of physical discomfort. I say 'eventually' because at the beginning of your recovery you might find you do need to sit through some physical discomfort as your body learns to accept nourishment again. This can be difficult and even emotionally painful, but try to keep focused on your end goal of health and well-being. It can also be useful to consistently remind yourself that just because you feel full, it doesn't mean that you have overeaten – rationalise with yourself that your body is just learning to be healthier and, as with all learning, it takes time. In many ways, you are going back to infancy and relearning the signals of the body and what they mean. Treat yourself with the same gentleness you would a child who is learning to recognise their bodily signals.

# The Seven Types of Hunger

During recovery, it might be easy for others to advise you to just keep on eating, but it is important to be mindful of when, what and how much you eat, as well as what type of hunger you are experiencing. There are actually seven types of hunger:[2]

1. **Nose hunger:** triggered by the wafting smells of food, such as popcorn at the cinema or freshly baked bread at a bakery. Scents can be very enticing.

2. **Eye hunger:** prompts you to eat upon seeing food that is visually appealing such as when a fast food advert plays on the television, when you see a restaurant's colourful and graphic menu, or when watching someone else eat. When we are visually stimulated to eat, we eat even when we are already full.

3. **Mouth hunger:** triggered when your palate is looking for a particular taste, flavour or texture. Even when you've eaten enough food, this hunger type can influence you to keep on searching for a particular kind of food that can satisfy the sensation your mouth is yearning for.

4. **Mind hunger:** prompted by thoughts and feelings that dictate what, when and how much to eat (or not eat), which do not necessarily align with what your body nutritionally needs. For people with anorexia, this could mean restricting certain foods because you believe you need to completely avoid fat – something that the body needs to survive. This kind of eating practice is often based on worry, rather than what the body needs. Mind hunger can only be managed once you learn to control your worries and anxieties, which will be discussed in Chapter 8.

5. **Heart hunger:** urges you to eat in order to deal with heightened emotions such as loneliness and sadness. When a person goes through a break-up or has a bad day, eating comfort foods can become an emotional escape. For people with anorexia, this desire to comfort eat can lead to so-called 'binges' followed by purging behaviour, or to further food restriction. Food restriction leads to a numbing of the heart hunger. Often in people with anorexia, hunger can actually be satisfied by starvation.

6. **Stomach hunger:** signals to the body that it is time to refuel. This kind of hunger usually does not pass easily and can lead to dizziness if not dealt with on time. The body has its own clock, and usually stomach hunger comes at regular intervals and at similar times each day. When a person is stomach hungry, the primary need is to find food rather than satisfy a specific craving.

7. **Cellular hunger:** triggered by the entire body when specific nutrients are lacking for it to function normally. Your body can tell you what you need. If you're feeling sluggish, you may need carbohydrates for energy. If you are feeling heavy and bloated, you might need more fibre from vegetables. If you're experiencing headaches and joint pains, you might be eating too much sugar or salt.

It isn't wrong to feel hunger – any type of hunger. Stomach hunger and cellular hunger are directly related to having a lack of food in the body. Recognising these two types is critical in re-feeding and re-nourishing your body. Additionally, experiencing the other types of hunger – nose, eye, mouth, mind and heart – is normal and can even encourage you to build a better appreciation for the different positive qualities of healthy food. It also emphasises the need to have variety and a range of smells, colours, flavours and textures in your diet plan.

Your body will need time to adjust to the changes in your eating habits, and it may become difficult to trust your hunger and fullness cues. Take the time to practise listening to your body – it is your body and isn't out to hurt you.

# Reintroducing Exercise

Many people with anorexia become obsessive with physical activity to the extent that they feel compelled to do it every day or at particular times of day. For me, recovery wasn't possible without me completely stopping exercise. At the beginning, I just couldn't associate exercise with anything other than weight loss and food restriction, so to get better I actually had to stop exercising. Then, as my mind and body started to heal, I could gently reintroduce it into my life – as a tool for health and well-being. Therefore, at the beginning of your journey to recovery, it may be necessary to postpone any engagement with exercise for a short period of time to get your thoughts together.[3]

If you do choose to take an exercise break and focus on your eating first, you might fear that getting back into exercise will pull you into the old habits and obsessions. While these fears and anxieties are valid, you need to start to develop a more positive perspective on physical activity. Physical activity is about more than weight – it is about health and taking care of yourself. Physical activity also helps us manage stress levels, moods, cravings and bodily functions. In this way, rather than being a tool to drive the anorexia, you can learn new ways of using exercise to help with recovery. First, however, consider using some of the following strategies to develop a healthier relationship with exercise:[4]

⇨ Seek advice from a personal trainer or expert on developing a personalised exercise plan based on your nutritional intake, physical well-being and mental health status.

⇨ Create a written contract with yourself or those supporting you as to how therapeutic exercise will be used, such as your goals, expectations and what you will do if you encounter any problems.

⇨ Learn about the non-weight-related benefits of physical activity.

⇨ Focus on how exercise supports your overall health and well-being (as opposed to weight loss).

⇨ Create a graded exercise programme, where you first learn to tolerate small amounts of exercise without overdoing things.

⇨ In the early stages of recovery, start with mild-intensity exercise to condition your body as you start to become physically stronger.

⇨ Tailor the mode of exercise to your needs, such as resistance training to help build strength or yoga to help encourage an appreciation of the body.

⇨ Include a nutritional component that ensures you are gaining the necessary nutrients to support the level of activity you are taking part in.

⇨ Debrief after every exercise session by assessing how the exercise made you feel physically and emotionally.

If it is not possible to achieve all of these strategies at the same time, try to slowly integrate them one by one into your health plan.

## Start with Friendly Group Activities

It's possible to get back into exercise by starting out with group activities where you can surround yourself with supportive health practitioners, friends and other people who may be on the same journey as you. Activities that are non-intimidating, relaxing and non-cardio such as walking, light weight lifting and yoga will help get your body moving while teaching you that you don't always have to push your body to extremes. One study found that yoga helps in reducing short-term preoccupations about food.[5] However, if you catch yourself thinking about using physical activity as an opportunity to burn calories, take a step back and reassess your intentions.

Taking part in physical activities with supportive people can also aid in creating a controlled social environment where you can discuss and process your goals, feelings, urges and thoughts.[6] Exercise becomes a social experience rather than an isolating experience. This is important in anorexia recovery, where both exercise and eating become lone activities. They don't have to be – they can be enjoyed in the company of others.

At the same time, don't force yourself into social activities if you aren't ready. I didn't like group activities as I was prone to comparing myself with others. Groups work for some, but not for everyone – and that is OK.

### Tips on how to exercise healthily

- Exercise for health and not for weight loss or fat burning.

- Introduce variety into your physical exercise plans to avoid being repetitive and reverting to a control-based mind-set.

- Try to choose physical activities that you can consider fun such as dancing or walking your dog.

- Be mindful and always try to establish a connection with your body.

- Be vigilant about urges to over-exercise, and stop yourself before the urge takes over.

Can you add any more?

# Promoting Recovery with Physical Activity

When selecting the best physical activity for you at various stages of your recovery, it can be useful to think of it in terms of elements other than weight. For example:

- physical activity that focuses on an appreciation of the body and its movements, such as yoga, dance and swimming

- physical activity that allows you to enjoy nature and get some fresh air, such as walking, cycling or gardening

- physical activity that involves time with animals, such as horse riding or walking your dog

- physical activity that is fun, such as trampolining, skipping rope or Frisbee.

Can you think of any more?

## Coping with Weight Gain

Another important aspect of physical well-being is achieving a healthy weight. Note the word 'healthy'. Recovery isn't about getting 'fat' – it is about being a healthy weight, a weight that allows you to function efficiently. As scary as it might sound, your body cannot fully recover if you are underweight and remain underweight. You might be asking, 'Is there any possible way to be healthier without gaining weight?' The answer is 'No'. Your body needs to create a layer that will protect your organs. You also need to build muscle to become stronger.

Weight gain is not something you need to fear, and I know that is easier said than done. Your mind might not let you believe this now, but give it time. A healthy mind will accept the need to be a healthy weight – and your mind will become healthier with every step you take towards recovery. Indeed, much of recovery is recognising that your thoughts and feelings might not be encouraging you to work towards recovery, and trusting that you are doing the right thing by overriding them. If you are underweight, weight gain is a sign that you are on your way towards getting your life back together. It isn't a sign that you are out of control. Far from it. It is a sign that you are finally in control.

Let your body reach a stable weight, which requires you to listen to your body's needs. You will naturally stop gaining weight once you have stabilised, as the body's focus will then shift from body repair and weight gain towards normalising metabolic activities.[7] Many people tend to relapse when they see that they have gained a little weight. You must prepare yourself mentally to be able to tolerate the added weight when the time comes. Indeed, it can be useful to have a plan of action in place even before you experience any weight gain. This will keep you focused and prevent you from resorting to the unhealthy ways of dealing with weight that you were using before you resolved to recover and regain your life.

It's normal to have a negative initial reaction to weight gain, and if there was ever a time you wanted to throw this book down, I suspect it is now. Be strong and recall why you are doing this. Try to focus on the better future you are working towards and remember that everything is in *your* time and when *you* are ready.

## Over to You!

Your physical recovery requires you to practise the ability to listen to your body – when it tells you it is hungry, full or in need of certain nutrients or physical activity. As hard as it will be at first, welcome the changes that your body will undergo – these are signs that you are on the right path. Start listening to your body by reflecting on the following questions.

✎ Practise identifying the seven types of hunger. In which situations do you typically experience each type? Also, recall an experience each for stomach hunger and cellular hunger. How did you decide what and how much to eat?

| Type of hunger | Situation/experience |
| --- | --- |
| Nose | |
| Eye | |
| Mouth | |
| Mind | |
| Heart | |
| Stomach | |
| Cellular | |

✎ What mild exercises are you confident you can include in your lifestyle plan? What are your plans to make these activities more fun and engaging?

| Exercise | How can I make these fun? |
|----------|---------------------------|
|          |                           |
|          |                           |
|          |                           |
|          |                           |
|          |                           |
|          |                           |
|          |                           |

✎ Weight gain can be a risk factor for relapse. Once you see a gradual increase in weight, what reminders will you give yourself to help manage the anxieties you might experience?

_____

_____

_____

_____

_____

_____

Remember that your long-term goal is to let your body recover and to take back control of your decisions and your life. Although difficult, reintroducing physical activities, responding to hunger cues and achieving a more stable weight are essential ingredients to your overall well-being. Indeed, taking control of your physical well-being will also help you take control of your psychological well-being, which is the topic of the next chapter.

# Chapter 8

# Taking Control of Your Psychological Well-Being

> *Emotions are not problems to be solved. They are signals to be interpreted.*
>
> Vironika Tugaleva

Your emotions and thoughts can strongly affect how you live your day-to-day life. Positive and healthy emotions, thoughts and beliefs are your shield against the vicious cycle of negative attitudes and behaviours often associated with anorexia. On the road to recovery, you will need to challenge some of the most deep-seated attitudes and beliefs you have about yourself and the way you treat yourself.

## Emotional Regulation

Strong and overwhelming emotions often contribute to both the onset and maintenance of anorexia. Research suggests there is a strong connection between anorexia and finding it difficult to regulate emotions.[1] In an attempt to control or compensate for overwhelming emotions such as anger, grief, frustration and depression, some people with anorexia translate their desire for control onto their eating habits and weight management practices. Indeed, in one study, people with anorexia perceived intense emotions like anger as threats that needed to be suppressed. Furthermore, this lack of emotional expression was linked to their heightened body dissatisfaction and drive for thinness.[2]

People with anorexia who successfully complete treatment show an improved ability to regulate their emotions.[3] However, managing your feelings in a healthy way is a skill that needs constant practice. It is easy to relapse into old, unhealthy eating habits once negative emotions start to creep in, which they will as part of the ups and downs of life.[4] Let's begin to explore your emotions to understand how easily they can take control over your decisions and behaviours.

## Feeling 'Fat'

Trying to control your food intake, weight and shape may provide temporary relief. After doing this for a prolonged period, however, you may end up at the mercy of the desire for control and perfection until such time that 'feeling thin' becomes the only equivalent to 'feeling better'.[5]

Consequently, many people with anorexia equate 'feeling fat' with 'being fat' — a feeling that fuels body dissatisfaction. This is because, with anorexia, feeling fat is a result of mislabelled and misunderstood emotions and experiences.[6] To this day, if I find myself feeling fat, I need to ask myself, 'What is really wrong?' There is always another explanation for this feeling and it more often than not indicates that I am not expressing my real emotions — be they sadness, anger or fear.

It is important to identify the triggers that make you feel fat, and how this sensation further spirals into other negative emotions. Some triggers for feeling fat are boredom, sadness, feeling bloated or simply eating. Even being hungry can make you feel fat!

Whenever you feel fat, try not to react immediately. Stop taking it as a cue to starve yourself or beat yourself up. Instead, sit with the sensation (as difficult as that may be) and try to investigate where the negative feeling is coming from.

## Positive Feelings with Bad Intentions

By exploring your emotions, you will start to see how all emotions — even the seemingly positive — can maintain anorexia-related habits. For example, losing weight and engaging in weight-loss behaviours can be very rewarding, and the positive feeling of achieving an anorexia-related goal can power your motivation to continue down the road of ill health.

Positive emotions are not the enemy here; rather, it is your interpretation of what constitutes an achievement. There is always the opportunity to harness the same level of positivity from other domains of your life – areas where you can also find motivation, experience autonomy and competency, and nurture an identity that is not defined by weight or shape.[7] For example, your personal passion or purpose is a fountain of motivation. Being 'in the zone' while doing something that is very meaningful to you can bring an intense level of positive feelings. Bring your awareness back to your greatest passion by asking yourself: What do I long to do with my life? By touching base with your deeper life purpose – whether it's writing, painting, singing, teaching or caring for animals – you gain a stronger drive to improve in these areas. Identifying other sources of positive emotions that are not rooted in weight or physical appearance is important. A better understanding of what constitutes success will become the springboard for setting healthier and happier goals.

## Express Yourself

Communication is key to your recovery. Many interventions for anorexia use the emotion-focused therapy (EFT) approach, which is designed to help you learn to communicate your emotions through a six-stage process:[8]

- **Recognise:** This is about learning to recognise when you are pushing your emotions down rather than dealing with them. It can help to be specific – for example, recognising that you are envious (specific) versus sad (generic), or that you are feeling a lack of fun in your life (specific) versus feeling empty (generic).

- **Monitor:** By monitoring your emotions and how you deal with them via a mood diary (see below), you can start to identify patterns and triggers for negative moods.

- **Express:** This is when you might feel the need to cry, write your feelings down, communicate your needs to someone or even scream out loud.

- **Accept:** Here you accept that your emotions are real, worthy and need to be taken care of.

- **Regulate:** As you develop the ability to recognise, monitor, express and accept your emotions, you can start to manage them better by developing the skills needed to deal with them.

- **Transform:** By naming your emotions and your needs, you will be empowered to transform a negative feeling into a solution (e.g. if you feel sad, you could spend time with someone who makes you happy).

Essentially, you need to start expressing emotions that you are used to pushing away or dismissing. In this way, you become more aware of them and start to reclaim them. Communicating with your counsellor or loved ones with honesty can help build your emotional intelligence (the capacity to be aware of, control and express your emotions), as well as improve your personal relationships. Just as eating is a natural and necessary behaviour for survival, so is emotional expression.

## Write It All Down

Increasing your awareness of intense feelings will gradually teach you how to regulate difficult emotions. Although unsettling at first, practising how to tolerate negative feelings will help you cope with life without having to turn to unhealthy methods of pushing your feelings away.[9] To document your emotions, keep a journal or write a letter to someone. You don't need to send the letter – just use it as a form of expression. You could even write the letter to yourself or to your inner child. The purpose of writing it all down is to help you recognise and process intense feelings, rather than allowing your emotions to control you.

Below is an example of a mood diary you could use to start monitoring your emotions and any related thoughts and behaviours, so that you can learn better methods of coping over time.

## Mood Diary

| Day & time | Mood/emotion (Rate intensity of emotion: 0–100%) | Comments (Example: What was happening, where, who with? What went through your mind (thoughts, images)? What were you doing just before and/or after you felt that way?) |
| --- | --- | --- |
|  |  |  |
|  |  |  |
|  |  |  |
|  |  |  |
|  |  |  |
|  |  |  |
|  |  |  |

*Source: Carol Vivyan[10]*

If you are more of a visual person, you could try the mood record below to understand what impacts your moods.

## Visual Mood Diary

| Monday | ☹ ☺ ☺ <br> 1  2  3  4  5  6  7  8  9  10 | + Good things today: <br> − Bad things today: |
|---|---|---|
| Tuesday | ☹ ☺ ☺ <br> 1  2  3  4  5  6  7  8  9  10 | + Good things today: <br> − Bad things today: |
| Wednesday | ☹ ☺ ☺ <br> 1  2  3  4  5  6  7  8  9  10 | + Good things today: <br> − Bad things today: |
| Thursday | ☹ ☺ ☺ <br> 1  2  3  4  5  6  7  8  9  10 | + Good things today: <br> − Bad things today: |
| Friday | ☹ ☺ ☺ <br> 1  2  3  4  5  6  7  8  9  10 | + Good things today: <br> − Bad things today: |
| Saturday | ☹ ☺ ☺ <br> 1  2  3  4  5  6  7  8  9  10 | + Good things today: <br> − Bad things today: |
| Sunday | ☹ ☺ ☺ <br> 1  2  3  4  5  6  7  8  9  10 | + Good things today: <br> − Bad things today: |

Source: Getselfhelp[11]

# Shifting Your Thoughts

Everyone is at risk of developing thinking habits that hinder rather than improve health and well-being. This is particularly common in people with anorexia. Negative thoughts can affect the anorexia just as powerfully as negative emotions. If done repeatedly, negative thinking creates a pathway in your mind, and whenever you are faced with overwhelming or unfavourable situations, you may tend to go down that ingrained pathway towards automatic negative mental responses.

Try to direct your awareness towards your mind and learn to identify your unconscious, unhealthy ways of thinking. Below are some examples of negative thinking styles to look out for. Do you recognise any of them in yourself? Tick all that apply.

☐ **Polarised thinking:** e.g. 'If I go beyond a certain weight, I'll be fat.'

This is about seeing things in extremes or in terms of black and white. Be kind to yourself and acknowledge that you are a complex person defined by more than a number on a weighing scale or a measuring tape.[12]

☐ **Labelling/mislabelling:** e.g. 'I'm an oversized pig.'

This is a harsh statement, but people with anorexia are harsh on themselves. Through labelling and mislabelling they will use one or two qualities or mistakes to define their entire being or that of another person. Using very negative words to define yourself doesn't lead to anything good. One mistake in the past does not define your actions in the future.[13]

☐ **Arbitrary inference:** e.g. 'Whenever I eat, I lose control. Therefore, I should avoid eating.'

This style of thinking is about jumping to often unfounded and overly critical conclusions. It involves expecting the worst in people, situations and yourself, and making decisions based on conclusions that are biased and emotionally charged.[14]

☐ **Overgeneralisation:** e.g. 'I can't do anything right.'

This is about applying a negative perception of yourself to every aspect of your life. Failing at one situation or event causes you to think that you are a failure in whatever else you do in life. This kind of thinking fuels negative emotions and further drives your desire to control overwhelming feelings (often through anorexia-related behaviours).[15]

When negative thinking has become an ingrained habit, you start to no longer recognise you are doing it. One way to get out of this habit is to start monitoring your thoughts.

# Monitor Your Thoughts

To break free from negative thought patterns, it can help to establish a way to monitor your thoughts. The goal is to become more mindful about the kind of thoughts you have and how they affect you emotionally, physically and behaviourally. Self-monitoring your thoughts can be achieved through journalling, just as with the mood diaries. Assessing how you think, whether positively or negatively, can further your understanding about your eating disorder and help you track your progress towards recovery. It can also supplement consultations with your counsellor or anyone else who is supporting you on your journey.[16]

The sheet below is an example of a thought record you might find useful when challenging your thoughts.

# Thought Record Sheet – Anorexia

| Situation | Emotions/moods (rate 0–100%) | Physical sensations | Unhelpful thoughts/images | Alternative/realistic thought or more balanced perspective | What I did/what I could do/defusion (distancing) technique/What's the best response? Re-rate emotion 0–100% |
|---|---|---|---|---|---|
| What happened? Where? When? Who with? How? | What emotion did I feel at the time? What else? How intense was it? | What did I notice in my body? Where did I feel it? | What went through my mind? What disturbed me? What did those thoughts/images/memories mean to me, or say about me or the situation? What am I responding to? What 'button' is this pressing for me? What would be the worst thing about that, or that could happen? | STOP! Take a breath... Is my reaction in proportion to the actual event? Am I underestimating my ability to cope? Am I mind-reading what others are thinking? Am I doing that 'compare & despair' thing? Am I misinterpreting that bloated feeling as fatness? Am I putting more pressure on myself? What would be more realistic? What would someone else say about this situation? What's the bigger picture? Is there another way of seeing it? What advice would I give someone else? | What will the consequences be of doing what I usually do? Is there another way of dealing with this? What could I do differently? What would be most effective? Do what works! Act wisely. What will be most helpful for me or the situation? |

Source: Carolyn Vivyan[17]

The STOPP strategy referred to in the thought record sheet can also be used outside of your monitoring record to help prevent any unrealistic thoughts from spiralling out of control:

⇨ **S**top!

⇨ **T**ake a breath.

⇨ **O**bserve your thoughts and feelings – what are they and how are they making me feel?

⇨ **P**ull back and put them into perspective – for example, is this thought a fact or opinion? Is there an alternative way of looking at it?

⇨ **P**ractise what works – what is the best thing to do right now, for both myself and others, as well as the situation?

## Challenging Your Beliefs

Your belief system determines how you look at a situation, how you act and how you interpret an experience in hindsight. Often, people with anorexia adhere to a set of beliefs that only serves to demolish their path to a healthy life. In cognitive behavioural therapy, discussed in Chapter 4, when a person learns to replace negative, unrealistic beliefs with more positive, realistic ones, they begin to alter their feelings, thoughts and behaviours in a favourable way.[18]

Together with your negative thoughts, start to challenge some of your unrealistic beliefs as well. Learn to identify your unhealthy beliefs and create a positive and realistic belief that stands in contrast to it.

## Turn your negative beliefs around

- Current belief system: 'If I'm not underweight, people won't love me.'

  Counter-belief: 'Those who love me want me to be healthy.'

- Current belief system: 'Eating is greedy.'

  Counter-belief: 'Eating is necessary; everyone needs to eat.'

- Current belief system: 'Putting on weight will make me hideous.'

  Counter-belief: 'Weight is just a number. My focus should be on getting my body to function healthily.'

- Current belief system: 'I cannot change. This is who I am.'

  Counter-belief: 'I know how to take better care of myself, even if I take it one day at a time.'

Add to these examples based on your own common and self-defeating beliefs.

To reduce your tendency to over-evaluate the importance of weight and shape, make a list of all the other aspects of your life, such as relationships, career, hobbies, self-discovery or other areas that might have taken a back seat due to your condition. Engage in these other domains and rediscover how important these are in your life.[19] From here, you can come up with positive beliefs that personally appeal to you. Anorexia invites negative thinking into your life, but you can be more positive just by changing your focus – from food and weight to living life to the full.

## Over to You!

By monitoring and evaluating your emotions, thoughts and beliefs, you will feel more in control of your recovery. You can challenge the negativity that has become an automatic response and gradually distance yourself from it. Over time, you will begin to see situations in a different, healthier and more positive way. Take the first few steps in confronting your negative feelings and thoughts by honestly answering the following questions:

✎ Take a notebook and monitor your feelings for the day. At what times do you 'feel fat'? Dig a little deeper. Where do you think the feeling is rooted? What was happening before that feeling emerged?

_____

_____

_____

_____

_____

_____

✎ Which unhealthy and negative thinking patterns do you think you have? Polarised thinking? Labelling/mislabelling? How do you plan to identify and challenge these?

_____

_____

_____

_____

_____

✎ What positive thoughts can you tell yourself to counter any negative beliefs you have about yourself or your body?

| My negative belief | My positive counter-belief |
|---|---|
|  |  |

✎ Taking anything related to weight out of the equation, what is important to you in life? Where could you direct your thinking in a healthier way?

_____

_____

_____

_____

_____

_____

Choosing to effectively monitor and evaluate your emotions, attitudes and beliefs towards food, weight and yourself will determine the success of your recovery. Don't be afraid of your feelings – just like hunger, they are there to help you. They are alerting you to an emotional need – by focusing on that emotional need, rather than pushing it away, you can start to try other, healthier ways to deal with the ups and downs of life.

# Chapter 9

# Taking Control of Your Social Well-Being

> *Together, life can bloom into something unimaginable!*
>
> Auliq-Ice

The recipe for a healthy and balanced life isn't complete without positive relationships. Without the support or mere presence of people you care about and who care about you, dealing with your internal battles will seem even more overwhelming. You don't need a lot of people in your life to gain from the benefits of social contact – in fact, it is the quality that matters much more than the quantity.

It is likely that as the anorexia progressed, you withdrew from social relationships for fear of being pressured to eat. However, it is likely that there are people in your life who are ready to listen and help – and, if this isn't the case, you can find them. This chapter will teach you how to distinguish the good relationships from the bad ones, how to better communicate with the people around you, and how to put relationships to good use in your recovery.

## Anorexia and Family Life

Many books will shy away from discussing the impact of family on anorexia through fear of passing blame. This isn't about passing blame, but about being realistic so that recovery becomes more attainable.

Research suggests that family challenges may contribute towards the onset and maintenance of anorexia. This is primarily because our family is our first interaction with the world and our first insight into relationships. It is where we develop our sense of self-worth and learn to look after ourselves. An unstable family life can shake our sense of safety and control, making us seek out that control elsewhere, such as via food and weight.

Some of the key links found between anorexia and family life include:

- Exposure to substance and alcohol abuse by family members increases the tendency to develop anorexia.[1]

- Developing an eating disorder is more common in families that emphasise competition and achievement, or lack open communication.[2]

- It is believed that mothers of daughters with anorexia may also have struggled with their own eating disorders.[3] *Indeed, anorexia is more likely in a family where the mother focuses on, and talks about, her own weight.*

- Anorexia is more widespread in families that are overly protective, rigid, perfectionistic and focused on success. There may also be an unhealthy focus on external rewards.[4]

- It is not uncommon to find that some individuals with eating disorders are from families that have experienced marital problems, divorce or domestic violence.[5]

- Not surprisingly, anorexia-related tendencies can surface after a family-related trauma, such as physical abuse, neglect or sexual abuse.[6]

## Enmeshment

A discussion of anorexia and family life wouldn't be complete without a look at enmeshment, which occurs when there is a loss of boundaries in a relationship. This is often the case in the mother/daughter relationship when the daughter is struggling with anorexia, but can also occur in other close relationships. It leads to a loss of sense of individuality in the person with anorexia, and taking control of the body becomes one way to grasp at autonomy and independence. Perhaps you recognise the feeling of not being able to separate your own identity from that of your mother, or another family member or carer. The lack of limits in the relationship gradually contribute to, and nurture, further enmeshment — until you don't know where you end and they begin.

Undoing years of enmeshment is an extremely slow and difficult process. Naturally, the first step is to acknowledge that there is a problem in the relationship and that it is impeding your recovery. Then you can begin the work of change. It is not unusual to feel uncertain about becoming independent from the person you are enmeshed with. Indeed, it can be scary to think about who you are, as a person, when you step outside of their powerful shadow. You might even feel a sense of betrayal towards them as you try to disentangle yourself. However, remind yourself of the importance of becoming your own person — of recognising your own needs and desires. Becoming independent is not a betrayal, but something natural.

## Family Roles

If you can recognise this sense of enmeshment, you might also be able to relate to being stuck in a family role that you feel has been imposed upon you. Indeed, anorexia can develop in families where certain roles are not performed or expressed in a healthy way. There are four general dysfunctional family roles:[7]

- **The Good Child:** Also known as the 'hero', this person appears to be 'perfect' in every way — successful, kind, responsible, capable and talented. This role can leave a person feeling that they can't meet the expectations others have of them. A constant pressure to be perfect can take its toll and hinder recovery.

- **The Scapegoat:** Also seen as a 'problem child', this member of the family can be labelled rebellious and a bit of a troublemaker. The 'problem' could simply be not fitting the same mould as the rest of the family, which can lead to any family problems being blamed on the scapegoat.

- **The Lost Child:** This is the quiet and somewhat isolated member of the family; in fact, so quiet, they are almost invisible to others. They tend to sacrifice their own needs and you will rarely hear them ask for anything. The Lost Child, also the Invisible Child, learns to take care of themselves and may eventually start to believe their needs aren't important. This is a belief that needs to be broken if anorexia is to be beaten.

- **The Mascot/Clown:** Also known as the 'joker', this is the member of the family who keeps tensions low and uses humour to deflect the family's attention away from problems. This might sound like a fun role to have, but it can lead to the person in this role masking any worries or negative feelings they have. Problems are pushed under the carpet rather than dealt with.

A person with anorexia can be placed into all of these roles and sometimes more than one. Once in a role, it can be difficult to escape it because everyone around you behaves in a way that keeps you in that role. Can you relate to any of these roles?

# Other Relationships

As well as relationships at home, members of your wider social circle can have an impact on the development and maintenance of your illness. Friends, for example, can pressure you into looking or behaving a certain way, whether that is their intention or not. Involvement in certain sports and activities such as ballet, modelling and swimming can also be a breeding ground for anorexia. You may be comparing yourself with other people in your team or group and thinking there is a high standard that you must adhere to. Romantic relationships are another potential factor in anorexia. You might feel pressured to constantly look attractive for your partner, or be self-conscious about being intimate.

Social media is playing an increasing role in our lives and has heightened our exposure to unrealistic standards of beauty. It has become a platform for people to compare themselves with other people who appear to have a 'perfect' life. This only leads to the development of unhealthy self-perceptions and unrealistic body image goals. Indeed, studies have found that the more time spent using social media platforms such as Facebook and Instagram, the higher the chances of developing a negative body image, low self-esteem and an eating disorder.[8]

Whatever relationships may be contributing to your illness, there is a deeper personal struggle with your body image, your insecurities and your self-esteem. You might be seeing your self-worth through the eyes of other people, based on how they have treated you.[9] To ensure the success of your recovery, you need to begin evaluating how your connections with other people are impacting you.

# Taking a Closer Look at Your Relationships

We can't change where we come from. We also can't change past experiences. However, we can take a closer look at the state of our personal relationships and reflect on how we might be able to improve them.

Research suggests that people with anorexia have difficulty managing certain domains of relationship functioning, such as communication, problem solving, conflict resolution and intimacy.[10] These domains are often shaped by how you were raised as a child, the experiences you had growing up and how you choose to respond to people during your adulthood. Fortunately, these interpersonal skills are not set in stone, and you can choose to work on them.

So, the initial step towards social well-being involves having the ability to identify the good relationships from the bad. Are your relationships healthy or toxic? Take a look at the list of characteristics of a healthy or unhealthy relationship below to find out:[11]

| Healthy relationships | Toxic relationships |
|---|---|
| Feel safe and secure. There is compassion and empathy. You have freedom to think and share your thoughts. You actively listen and are actively heard. There is mutual caring and genuine concern. There is respect despite differences in opinion. | Feel unsafe and insecure. There is abuse of power or authority. Some choices made are self-serving and demanding of the other person. There is an aura of negativity and distrust. Demeaning comments are commonly said and heard. There is jealousy and dishonesty. |

## Evaluate your relationships with these questions:

- Does this relationship energise me or does it drain me?

- Do I feel negative about myself when around this person due to comments they make?

- Does the other person pressure me to look or be a certain way?

- Am I confident that this relationship will support me in my recovery?

## Positive Relationships and Recovery

The strong impact that members in your social circle have on your overall well-being indicates that you need to evaluate every relationship in your life. This will help you come to terms with the fact that those relationships that you find to be unhealthy might need to change, or some may even need to stop. Once you have identified which connections are healthy and which are not, focus on building those positive relationships – you are worth it.

Rebuilding lost friendships that might have been damaged during the height of your illness is also something you might want to consider. In making up for lost time, you might need to discuss what went wrong. This means that before accepting help from others, it helps to be honest and explain to them the background of the disorder. In this way, friends and family members can have a better understanding of what might help or hinder your recovery. For those friends and family you trust the most, you might even want to share this book with them so that they can gain a better understanding of your needs.

## Knowing When to Say Goodbye

Recovery is a time for new beginnings. Unfortunately, certain unhealthy relationships that are unlikely to change may need to be eliminated from your life. People who are inherently negative or domineering may not be a positive influence or a good fit during your recovery period.[12] You might need to stay away from them temporarily or decide to cut them off permanently. I cut myself off entirely from some of my family as I knew recovery was impossible with them in my life. I always felt bad around them, and my way of coping with that low sense of self-worth was to turn to disordered eating behaviours. This wasn't an easy decision and it took years for me to take the step I did. This isn't to say that you need to cut ties with people, but do think about who you want to spend more time with versus those you might want to spend less time with. Who supports your long-term goals?

## Over to You!

This chapter has described how to take a closer look at your relationships and the role of these relationships in your recovery. Some relationships may have very deep foundations in your life and can no longer be changed. However, you have the power to build your understanding of how various relationships influence your illness and focus on the positive relationships. Complete the tasks below to help you get started.

✎ Do you fit any of the family roles described in this chapter (Good Child, Lost Child, Mascot, Scapegoat)? If so, how does it make you feel and is this something you would like to change? If so, how could you go about making that change?

_____

_____

_____

_____

_____

_____

✎ Reflect on the relationships that are significant to you but do not possess the characteristics of a healthy and positive relationship. In what ways do these relationships affect how you feel about yourself and how you respond to social situations? Do they need to change? If so, how do you plan to improve them?

_____

_____

_____

_____

_____

_____

✎ **Make a list of the positive relationships in your life and how they improve your world.**

| I have positive relationships with... | They improve my life by... |
| --- | --- |
| | |
| | |
| | |
| | |
| | |
| | |

Meaningful and happy relationships are those where the people involved do not intend to control the other person. They are open, accepting and filled with care. You deserve to be around people who are loving, have good intentions for you, and want to see you get better.

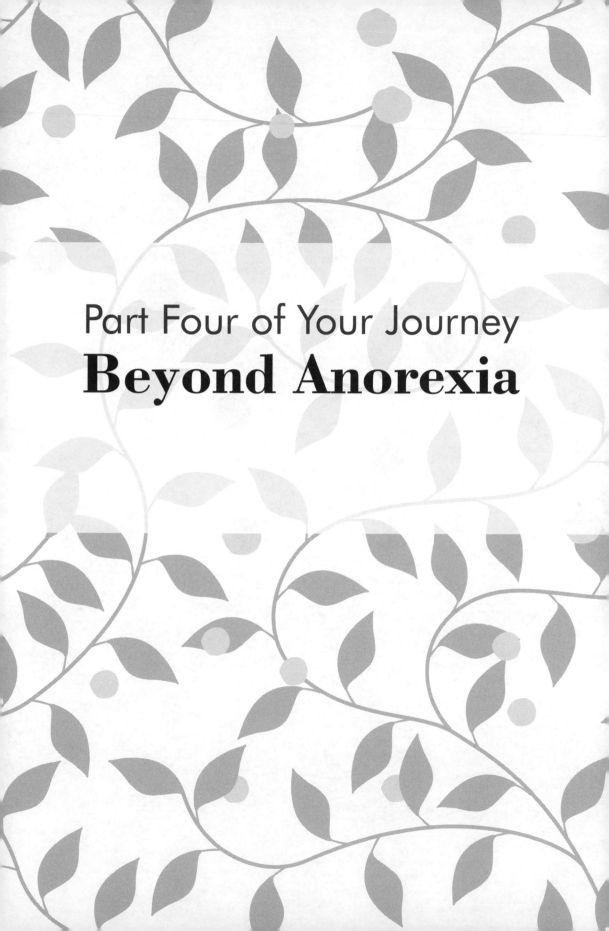

Part Four of Your Journey
# Beyond Anorexia

# Chapter 10

# Accepting Yourself

> *The curious paradox is that when I accept myself just as I am, then I can change.*
>
> Carl Rogers

The road to full recovery from anorexia is paved with many important aspects of healing the body and mind, as well as learning to have healthy relationships – but even more important is accepting yourself. The aim of this chapter is to help you start to do just that. Accepting yourself will help you maintain your recovery, while also cultivating an attitude of appreciation and reducing emotions and thinking patterns that can lead to relapse.

## Self-Acceptance: The Foundation of Recovery

Accepting who you were and who you are now as a result of the work you've done in recovery is fundamental to long-term stability and mental health. Just as accepting your illness and admitting your anorexia has been instrumental in initiating recovery, accepting who you are *without* anorexia is fundamental to long-term success in remaining free from unhealthy behaviours. Accepting the physical body and any changes in weight and shape will present challenges, but you have got this far in your journey and have already probably achieved things you didn't think you could.

Depending on your family of origin, your life experiences, your temperament and where you are in your recovery journey, you will likely experience self-acceptance to varying degrees. You may find that you experience limited self-acceptance or the ability to accept certain aspects of yourself but not others. Wherever you are on your path, self-acceptance is a practice you can cultivate and eventually master with the right tools.

So, what exactly is true self-acceptance? Self-acceptance is defined as the ability to accept all of your personal attributes, whether positive or negative. Self-acceptance means not judging your actions, thoughts or feelings, and not defining your value by any external criteria, including your weight or whether or not you are accepted by others.[1] Self-acceptance means accepting your physical body, your needs and your emotions. Acceptance is not about approval or disapproval but rather allowing 'what is' without judgement.[2] Being in a state of self-acceptance does not mean accepting low standards of health or resigning yourself to living with anorexia or anything else that is problematic. On the contrary, true self-acceptance allows you to bring about change in a loving, self-compassionate and lasting manner.

## Actively Cultivating Self-Acceptance

If self-acceptance seems like a foreign concept to you, do not despair! Begin your process of learning to accept yourself by accepting the fact that you don't feel accepting of yourself. Stopping judgement of yourself (and others) is a fundamental aspect of acceptance, so beginning exactly where you are without labelling yourself 'good' or 'bad' is an excellent place to start. The more you practise self-acceptance, the more natural it becomes. Here are some ways you can cultivate self-acceptance:

⇨ **Avoid judging.** Constantly judging ourselves and others is a way of rejecting reality. When you find yourself casting judgement of any sort, pause and try to notice exactly what you're doing. Perhaps you're evaluating a meal in which you ate a potentially triggering food. You find yourself saying things such as 'It's bad that I ate that food because it is "fattening"' or 'I am hungry so often I must be greedy.' With practice, you can transform judgement to awareness by shifting the inner dialogue to 'I *notice* that I am *telling* myself I should not have eaten this food and that I am bad for having eaten it' or 'I ate this food. I feel…about having eaten this food.' When you stop judging yourself in such an extreme way, you can begin to understand your actions and emotions and to see them as neither 'good' nor 'bad', which will then give you the space to devise better ways to care for yourself.

⇨ **Eliminate 'shoulds'.** When we constantly tell ourselves what we 'should' and 'shouldn't' do, feel, be, say or want, we reject the person we truly are. Often, this is a learned behaviour our parents unintentionally taught us that feeds disordered thinking and behaviour. When you catch yourself saying things like 'I should do this' or 'I shouldn't do that', recognise that you are probably resisting a need. Instead of beating yourself up, gently and objectively investigate what is beneath these harsh statements of self-rejection. It is likely that you will uncover aspects of yourself that you feel you must reject because you find them too painful or overwhelming to process. If you can look at these parts with curiosity, you can begin to accept yourself and identify and change limiting beliefs that are holding you back from being who you truly are.

⇨ **Observe yourself from a distance.** While it may sound contradictory, one way you can learn to accept yourself is to practise observing yourself from an outside or neutral position. Another way of thinking about this concept is 'separating the actor from the action'. This does not mean disconnecting from yourself but rather looking at yourself, your feelings and your actions without casting judgement, labelling or becoming the experience you are having. Think of how a video camera would capture you or how an objective observer would describe you. For example, if you find yourself feeling infuriated, it can be easy to get caught up in the emotion and to identify with the emotion by thinking or saying, 'I *am* angry,' and taking an 'angry' action. Instead, practise observing yourself when you *have* angry *feelings*; from this more neutral place you can begin to look at what triggered your emotions and thoughts and to understand your response to them from a place of acceptance. Moving into a place of acceptance of your experiences and your emotional responses to them will help you cultivate acceptance of yourself and what is happening.

# Self-Acceptance and Body Image

Anorexia is a battle with the body and part of recovery will be accepting your body and learning to value and nurture it. Many people with anorexia also struggle with body dysmorphic disorder (BDD), which can make self-acceptance of the body feel impossible. BDD is a condition whereby the person is preoccupied with their image, specifically with any perceived flaws in their appearance. This leads to an urge to continuously check their appearance, frequently seek reassurance from others, check for skin defects, skin pick to try to make their skin smoother, and constantly compare themselves to others. It is a very time-consuming condition and leads to a distorted self-image because the person fixates on 'defects' – many of which don't exist or are negligible. Nothing but flaws are noticed and the person is, in many ways, 'body blind'.

Your negative and distorted body image might be one of the last things to be resolved, and if you also have BDD, you might need extra support for this in the form of cognitive behavioural therapy (see Chapter 4). There are, however, some steps you can take to help cultivate a positive relationship with your body:

⇨ Avoid reading magazines that encourage you to compare yourself to others.

⇨ Dress in clothes that make you feel comfortable and confident, and that bring out your personality.

⇨ Send messages of appreciation and gratitude to aspects/parts of your body you are happy with.

⇨ Engage in activities that allow you to shift energy, use your muscles and enjoy your body, such as yoga, gardening, walking and meditating.

⇨ Practise appreciating your body for what it does for you, such as allowing you to walk, digest food, enjoy playing with your pet.

⇨ When you look in the mirror, tell yourself, 'I like who I am' and 'I like the way I look,' even if you don't yet believe this – say those things you are aiming to be able to say in the future.

## Building Your Self-Esteem and Self-Worth

Building your self-esteem and sense of self-worth will help you to maintain the progress you have made so far and continue your journey to even better health. Affirmations can help you in this endeavour by transforming the way you see and feel about yourself and your life. Affirmations work on the inner aspects of ourselves – our self-talk and the beliefs that govern how we live, think and feel about who we are and what happens in the world. At first, it may seem that affirmations are superficial or ineffective, but, over time, repeating the right affirmations can have lasting and profound effects. However, if you want affirmations to work, you do need to create an environment in which these new ideas can thrive – an environment where others support your affirmations and where you are willing to repeat them daily.

Finding affirmations that have personal meaning for you is key; this is best done by listening to your intuition and noticing how you feel when you say a particular affirmation. If the words feel good, keep repeating them. If they don't, create statements of your own that speak your truth. Here are some affirmations to get you started:

- 'I am enough.'

- 'I am worthy of love, belonging and acceptance.'

- 'My thoughts, feelings, desires and needs matter.'

- 'I am so much more than my weight.'

- 'I love myself and my body.'

- 'I am supported and loved.'

As with self-acceptance and body image, you might need to start this practice without a belief in what you are saying. If you can believe it straight away, this is great, but if (like some) you don't have any positive words to say to yourself, start out by acting. I use the word 'act' because in order for the affirmations to eventually resonate, you need to own them. Until you can say them with genuine belief, act as though you are someone who does genuinely believe them. Many of the tasks within this book are about reprogramming your brain. It has become immersed in the anorexia and now needs your tender, loving care.

## Give Yourself Self-Acknowledgement

If you find it difficult to be kind to yourself and keep finding reasons not to say positive words to yourself, start with something objective – something you can't deny deserves some acknowledgment. For example, what about the progress you have made regarding your recovery and other areas of your life? Even picking up this book and making it to this chapter deserves acknowledgement.

From here, you could integrate a daily 'self-acknowledgement' practice into your routine as a great way to focus on your strengths and abilities, as well as to build your sense of self-worth. Celebrating simple achievements, even small tasks, strengthens motivation to practise self-care and creates both positive feelings and an optimistic attitude. This will have both immediate and lasting effects on your physical and mental health, as positive emotions can support resiliency. Maintaining emotional buoyancy also helps you prevent and endure any setbacks or relapses without giving up. Your self-acknowledgement practice can be combined with other daily self-care rituals and used as a self-help tool to combat anxiety when you feel you are falling behind or unable to finish the tasks life has placed in front of you.

## Over to You!

✎ Take out your journal or a piece of paper and write down ten things you accomplished today. Include menial tasks such as loading the dishwasher, self-care and mindful eating, as well as routine duties like walking the dog or attending class or work.

1. _____

_____

2. _____

_____

3. _____

_____

4. _____

_____

5. _____

_____

6. _____
   _____

7. _____
   _____

8. _____
   _____

9. _____
   _____

10. _____
    _____

Notice if you feel the urge to minimise or judge what you've accomplished or have the desire to omit certain accomplishments from your list because you think they 'don't matter'. Remember, no task is too insignificant to be added to the list! When you've completed your list, spend a few minutes celebrating each item you've written down. Allow yourself to feel truly good about what you've accomplished. Do this daily for optimal results. You are retraining your brain and, like all training, this requires practice.

✎ **Devise ten affirmations that will help you build your self-esteem and sense of self-worth. If you can't come up with ten now, come back the next day and the next – until you have ten. Repeat each affirmation to yourself at least once a day – more if possible. Stick them up on your wall or carry them around in your pocket or bag as a reminder.**

1. _____

   _____

2. _____

   _____

3. _____

   _____

4. _____

   _____

5. _____

   _____

6. _____

   _____

7. _____

   _____

8. _____

   _____

9. _____

   _____

10. _____

    _____

✎ List five aspects of your body that you like and why. Remember that this isn't about appearance, but about what these aspects of your body help you achieve in your daily life.

1. _____
   _____

2. _____
   _____

3. _____
   _____

4. _____
   _____

5. _____
   _____

Now that you are armed with some tools to help you nurture the way you feel about yourself, let's take a look at your future, which will be much more pleasant if you like – or even love – yourself.

# Chapter 11

# Your Future Is in Your Hands

> The vast possibilities of our great future will become realities only if we make ourselves, in a sense, responsible for that future.
>
> Gifford Pinchot

Undoubtedly, anorexia is a condition that limits your potential for achievement, happiness and personal fulfilment. It can take away precious months or years of your life that can never be given back. However, by reaching out for help and tackling your condition head on, the barriers to reaching your full potential slowly break down. You have a new and exciting start ahead of you – and you can do what you want with it!

## Maintaining the New You

While turning to others and asking for their assistance is the right thing to do as you embark on recovery, to sustain recovery you need to create a new life beyond anorexia. Remember the stages of readiness to change discussed in Chapter 5 – pre-contemplation, contemplation, preparation, action, maintenance? You are now in Stage 5, maintenance of all of the positive changes you have made so far.

This doesn't mean forgetting about your plight with the condition. Indeed, your battle to beat anorexia can be turned into a strength and a reminder of all that you can achieve if you put your mind to it. Moving beyond anorexia is about replacing the anorexia with a new challenge – one that is about achieving your dreams and aspirations, and utilising your new-found health and freedom to create a life you want.

# Setting Inspirational Ambitions

Anorexia probably took over your life to the point that you began to think that the illness was part and parcel of your identity. In setting fresh new goals and defining ambitions, the general aim is to retrieve and redefine your identity. The goals you set to motivate yourself should not be limited to food, but should be broader and about your future rather than your present. It is important to put a spotlight on other areas of life and to bring passion and purpose into them so that you have plenty to look forward to.[1]

As the architect of your future, you can design it to be more balanced than it was when you were struggling with anorexia. Such balance involves distributing your attention between those areas of life that you value, such as relationships, family, health, education, personal development, financial success and career, to name a few. Some examples of ambitions relating to some major life areas are:

- **Health:** Health goals might include getting more vitamin D, maximising rest from sleep, eating more fruit and practising relaxation or meditation each morning.

- **Relationships and family:** Some relationship goals include spending more time with family, creating more meaningful conversations with your partner, making new friends.

- **Personal development:** Some examples of what you can do to achieve personal development include taking part in activities that are outside your comfort zone occasionally, such as travelling or tackling a fear that you want to overcome.

- **Career and business:** Some career goals to consider are determining the career that means most to you, achieving work–life balance, earning a promotion or resigning and starting your own business, to name a few.

- **Education:** Maybe you have always wanted to complete a degree, enrol in higher education or learn about new topics. Now is your chance.

- **Creativity:** Creativity goals could include learning a new language, joining an art class, cooking, blogging or taking up a craft.

To help sustain your desire to stay healthy and fulfil the aspirations you have set yourself, you might sometimes need to take a step back and ask yourself the following questions:

- What will motivate me to keep on going?

- Which aspirations will I no longer be able to pursue if I don't stay healthy?

- Visually, what do my aspirations look like compared with the alternative of relapse?

- How will relapse affect my dreams?

- How important are my dreams and aspirations to me?

Are there any other questions that can help keep you on track with your recovery and your pursuit of the future you desire?

## Defining Your Goals and Enjoying the Process

Success at anything is a process, not an event. Achieving one goal is fantastic, but it doesn't end there. Once old goals are met, new ones can be set. Indeed, constantly setting new goals allows you to develop a commitment to yourself and your life.

The first step in the process is defining your goals. Here, a five-year or ten-year vision of yourself creates the big picture of your life – are you making your way there? Having no clear goals can make you lose your way, but setting ambitions for yourself makes you accountable for what you do today. The question 'Will this help me become the person I always envisioned myself to be?' will help clarify which choices you want to be making each day.

Goals need to be manageable and appropriate to the context of a balanced and happy life. Ambitions also need to be reasonable: not impossible, but also not too easy. The key is setting specific, measurable, attainable, realistic and timely (SMART) goals:

⇨ **Specific:** Identify the who, what, when, where and why of your goal.

⇨ **Measurable:** Set criteria that can be used to assess progress and determine whether the goals have in fact been met.

⇨ **Attainable:** Match your goals with your ability, drive and resources (do not under- or over-estimate what you can do) to sustain a healthy mental momentum towards achieving the goal.

⇨ **Relevant:** Ensure that the goal springs from your personal values and suits your life and not someone else's.

⇨ **Timely:** Set a deadline you can work towards. This ensures you take actions.

Goals should not be unrealistic expectations, which can compromise your principles and personal values, ability for self-care, relationships or self-esteem.[2] When a setback happens, which is normal during anorexia recovery, unreasonable goals can lower your confidence and carry you back into an emotional downward spiral. Hence, setting unreasonable goals will only create an unnecessary emotional trap that you do not need or deserve. Anorexia is the ultimate unrealistic goal – attempting to deny yourself the necessity of food and linking happiness to a certain weight; neither of these are achievable, even if the illness tries to convince you that they are.

# Relapse Prevention

Relapse prevention strategies will go a long way in helping you stay on track as you pursue goals and ambitions beyond anorexia. So, while you now want to focus on a life without the illness, you don't want to leave yourself vulnerable to it sneaking back in. So, first and foremost, be aware of relapse warning signs. These include:

- thoughts and behaviours becoming focused on food, weight and dieting

- avoidance of certain foods, food groups or nutrients

- recurrence of rigid eating patterns related to time, location and quantity.

- withdrawal from other people

- depression and/or anxiety

- dishonesty with loved ones about what you have or haven't eaten

- secretive behaviours

- looking in the mirror often, primarily to criticise yourself

- feeling ashamed after eating

- avoidance of events involving food

- exercising to look good rather than to be healthy

- excessive preoccupation with perfection

- obsessive weighing.

If you spot any of these alarm bells, you need a 'relapse prevention plan' to turn to. This is something to devise even before these alarm bells are raised and which will tell you what to do if you feel you might be relapsing. In particular, your relapse prevention plan will answer the following questions at a time when you might not be able to effectively establish solutions to your problems:

- Which of the tools I learned during my recovery can I utilise now? For example, if you are struggling with irrational beliefs about yourself, maybe you can employ the counter-belief strategy discussed in Chapter 8? If you are having difficulty with urges to restrict your food, maybe you can return to keeping a food diary (Chapter 6) to determine the underlying triggers?

- What type of support do I need – informational, emotional, practical? (See Chapter 3.) Where can I get this support from?

- Which health professionals can I turn to if needed and what are their contact details?

- What self-affirmations will help motivate me to stay on the recovery track?

- How can I look after myself and provide self-care during this time? Do I need to comfort my inner child (Chapter 4) or release my emotions through writing or art (Chapter 8)?

- What chapters of various books will help me re-establish my recovery focus?

Importantly, don't see relapse risk or even total relapse as failure but as an indication that your recovery plan needs to be modified and re-evaluated.[3] Indeed, once you have worked out what triggered you, add a new relapse prevention strategy to your relapse prevention plan to account for similar potential triggers. A sample relapse prevention plan can be found in the appendix, along with a template you can complete for your own relapse prevention needs.

Also, remember that a 'slip' or a 'lapse' is very different from full-blown relapse. A slip in anorexia recovery is an unexpected 'fall' that you can come back from. A lapse is a mistake made because of inattention — maybe you put yourself in a triggering situation before you were ready. Slips and lapses aren't the end of the world and aren't an opportunity to beat yourself up. In fact, they are part of your learning process as you develop new skills and abilities to beat anorexia.

A relapse is a return of symptoms after a period of stabilised improvement. While it is more serious than a slip or a lapse, it still isn't the end of the world. It doesn't negate all the hard work you have done towards your recovery and it doesn't suddenly make all of your positive changes worthless. Why? Because you are still further along your recovery journey than you were. You have new skills, new tools, and evidence that you can change your behaviour for the better. Relapse means you did manage to achieve a healthier behaviour; your difficulty was maintaining that change. That is something you can continue to work on. In many ways, recovery is ongoing and isn't about getting from A to B. It is about ongoing growth and self-development in various areas of your life.

## Over to You!

This chapter has provided encouragement for you to search for possible ambitions or goals that might help sustain your desire to stay healthy. Complete the following exercises to draw inspiration as you begin to design your future.

✎ Defining your personal values will help lay the groundwork for setting your goals and ambitions. So, what does your best possible future look like? What will it take to get there? What do you currently have within your skillset or personality to help get you there?

_____

_____

_____

_____

_____

✎ As the true architect of your future, what specific, measurable, attainable, relevant and timely (SMART) goal do you want to achieve in each of these areas of life?

| Area of life | SMART Goal |
| --- | --- |
| Health | |
| Profession/Education | |
| Relationships | |
| Hobbies | |
| Creativity | |
| Travel | |
| | |
| | |
| | |

Add any other areas of life that are important to you in the space provided and think of a SMART goal for these too.

✎ **Create a vision board of your aspirations – this is a board that you fill with pictures of your goals. What will your vision board look like? What activities will be on it? How will you maintain it or mark when an aspiration has been achieved?**

_____

_____

_____

_____

_____

✎ **What other tools are there to keep your desire for a better and more balanced life strong and filled with inspiration?**

_____

_____

_____

_____

_____

Life offers so many possibilities and it is time to explore them.

# This Is Your Beginning

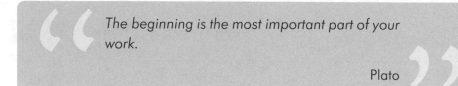

> *The beginning is the most important part of your work.*
>
> Plato

Congratulations on completing this workbook! If you have really engaged with this workbook and given it your all, you will have been on a journey. It will have been a tough journey, with many twists and turns, but you have made it this far. And guess what? This isn't the end. It is only the beginning and you can choose where your new path will take you.

You might find you need to revisit various chapters of this workbook to keep you on track, and that is fine. This is what this workbook is there for – a companion to help you live the life you want and deserve – happy and healthy. You have so much to look forward to, if you allow yourself.

As we come to this juncture, I would like to wish you the very best as you embark on your new beginning – a new beginning which I hope will be enhanced by the tools you have gained from this workbook, especially the tool of self-care.

## Good Luck and Good Health – You Can Beat Anorexia!

# Part Five
# **Advice for Family and Friends**

If you have picked up this book or been given it by a loved one, then you are in a privileged position. Either way, you are an important part of someone's life. That someone has been struggling with a very serious condition – anorexia – but has taken huge strides towards recovery. Even reading this book needs to be acknowledged as a huge achievement for them.

Now, they need your love and support. First, to embark on their recovery journey and then to maintain recovery. This might seem overwhelming for you, but there are some key steps you can take to be there for your loved one. Read on to find out what these steps are.

Chapter 12

# Helping a Loved One Recover – Effective Communication

> "
> *Communication to a relationship is like oxygen to life.*
>
> Tony Gaskins
> "

Good communication between the person with anorexia and their family and friends can help reduce any anxiety they might have about recovery. It might be difficult for you to contemplate that anyone would have anxiety about escaping an illness, but you need to understand that this is a very real anxiety for those with anorexia. The illness has become part of their identity, as well as their primary coping tool. Recovery can feel like the rug is being taken from underneath them and that their self-identity is being destroyed. And, yes, sometimes when you are trying to help, they will feel as if you are trying to hurt them. Your support can feel like a threat, so don't take it personally if your loved one is resistant – or even angry – about your efforts to help them.

Anorexia is very much a form of communication, or a sign that a person has difficulty communicating their thoughts, feelings and needs. So, if you want to help someone with recovery, it is necessary to understand the type of communication that helps versus the type that doesn't help. This chapter provides such an understanding, including practical examples of how to deal with mealtimes and how to send the right messages to your loved one about food and weight.

# Mealtimes

Mealtimes can be rife with emotions in a household where someone has anorexia, and you aren't alone if you just don't know how to be with your loved one during eating occasions. One thing to remember is that however difficult mealtimes are for you, they are a million times more difficult for your loved one. They are likely to be feeling anxious, fearful and guilty about consuming food. Although you can't take these feelings away, you can help by taking steps to normalise eating. If the focus of mealtimes becomes the anorexia, your loved one (and you) will feel even more anxiety at these times. Instead, reduce mealtime anxiety by following some of these guidelines for before, during and after meals:

- Before meals:

  ⇨ **Plan ahead.** Anxiety can be relieved if, together, you and your loved one agree on what mealtimes are all about, including times, the type of food, portion sizes, who will be present, and anything else that you both feel is key to making mealtimes less stressful.

  ⇨ **Set realistic goals,** such as introducing one new food per week to prevent your loved one staying 'stuck' in their recovery by only eating certain food groups.

- During meals:

  ⇨ **Avoid talking about food and weight.** Instead, try to keep the conversation on less emotional topics, such as how the day has been or what you have planned for the days ahead.

  ⇨ **Don't focus on the person with anorexia.** Everyone needs to be included in any conversations so that your loved one doesn't feel singled out.

  ⇨ **Provide distraction.** This can be achieved by talking about anything other than what is being eaten. Other strategies include having some background music on, or even the radio or television.

  ⇨ **Eat nutritionally balanced meals.** Model the type of eating you would wish for your loved one, including a variety of healthy and nutritious foods.

⇨ **Provide encouragement.** You might sometimes need to focus on food by encouraging your loved one to eat. Acknowledge that you understand their difficulties, while also being firm that eating is important.

⇨ **Take it slowly.** Someone with anorexia will have two major struggles to overcome when reintroducing normal eating – not only will they be fighting guilt and fear, but on a physical level they won't be able to eat as much as others because their stomach will have shrunk. Don't expect full meals to be eaten straight away – it is a slow and gradual process, and acknowledgment of even small improvements is deserved.

• After meals:

⇨ **Be active** – not necessarily physically, but *do* something with your loved one – go for a walk, watch a film, play a game. Such distractions will prevent compensatory behaviours such as over-exercising, vomiting or laxative use – all of which result from the guilt or panic of eating.

⇨ **Offer empathy.** If your loved one is struggling, acknowledge this and show understanding of their fears and anxieties. Ask if you can do anything to help.

Even when following these guidelines, mealtimes may feel like a battlefield. They will be difficult and draining for all involved. Try to accept this. It is a long process that can't be rushed.

# Sending the Right Messages

Effective communication with your loved one isn't just about food and weight. Thinking about how you communicate outside of the anorexia is also important:

⇨ Express value for your loved one in terms of who they are as a person, not just what they look like or what they do. This might sound obvious, but it is surprising how much emphasis many of us place on appearance and actions compared with simply having someone in our life. Replace comments about appearance with acknowledgement of achievements or personality traits that you appreciate. Is your loved one kind, creative or adventurous? Notice these aspects of them out loud and demonstrate that there is more to someone than what they look like on the outside.

⇨ Don't make assumptions about what your loved one is thinking or feeling. Ask. Even when life seems to be going well, taking the time to ask your loved one how they are shows that you care about their well-being. You might show you care in many other ways, but opening communication so that your loved one can express their needs in their own words will go a long way in making them feel cared for. Sometimes *showing* we care isn't enough, and we need to check that the care we are expressing is being *felt*.

Be consistent with the messages of love and support you provide your loved one. Even when times are rocky and even if you lose your patience from time to time, remain steadfast in your support and your strong desire for your loved one to get better. Indeed, be honest if you need to step away and gather yourself before discussing a concern with your loved one. This demonstrates your needs and mirrors to your loved one that it is OK to have needs. It also demonstrates that positive communication can remain strong even when situations are difficult. The key message is to communicate and to allow your loved one to communicate too.

# Chapter 13

# Breaking Free from Family Roles

> " *One of the symptoms of being free is you begin to dream.*
>
> Danny Silk "

A family is greater than the sum of its parts; liken it to a baby's mobile – when one piece moves, the whole mobile moves. In other words, one family member affects the whole family. Taking a close, honest look at the roles within your family – those that are healthy and those less healthy – will be an important part of your loved one's recovery. This isn't about passing blame onto the family for your loved one's illness, but exploring how this very important unit in their life could better support their health through change.

## Family Roles

Every family is made up of specific 'roles' and this applies with or without anorexia in the family. For example, you might be the 'caretaker' and someone else the 'breadwinner'. You might be the 'emotional' one and someone else the 'practical' one. When it comes to the person with anorexia, it is likely that for some reason or other they have adopted a dysfunctional role that could be preventing them from full recovery. These roles were discussed in Chapter 9 to help your loved one think about their role within the family. Briefly, these dysfunctional roles include:

- **The Good Child:** The person who appears to be 'perfect' in every way, leaving them feeling that they can't meet the expectations others have of them.

- **The Scapegoat:** The person who doesn't fit into the family mould, leading to many family problems being blamed on them.

- **The Lost Child:** The quiet and somewhat isolated member of the family who sacrifices their own needs for others, eventually believing their needs aren't important.

- **The Mascot/Clown:** The member of the family who keeps tensions low through humour and distraction, leading them to mask any problems they have.

Does your loved one fit into any of these roles? Fortunately, this doesn't have to be a disadvantage and can be used to help your loved one recover. Indeed, family systems theory states that no one can be understood in isolation and that in order to understand someone, we also need to understand their family system.[1] Simply by identifying someone's role in your family, if it is an unhealthy role, you can help them break free from it. Family roles are difficult to change because they are so ingrained; however, if everyone in a family can understand their individual roles, they can better help their loved one break free from any role that might hinder recovery.

So, now that you have identified your loved one's family role, what about your own? Maybe you can relate to one of the roles discussed? Alternatively, some other roles and traits that might resonate with you or which you might see in other family members are outlined below. Be honest when considering these family roles; it will help give your loved one the best chance of recovery.

- **The Socially Conscious One:** This is the family member who works to hide any family problems from those outside the family unit, often out of a sense of shame. This can make the person with anorexia feel that this family member is embarrassed by them. It also sends the message that we must be a certain way in order to be seen as acceptable.

- **The Troubled Person:** This is the troublemaker of the family who uses behaviour that is seen as unacceptable to deflect attention away from the real issues. This can lead to all of the attention being placed on the person who is explicitly acting out, pushing the person with anorexia into the background.

- **The Rescuer:** This is the hallmark trait of 'the Enabler', who desperately tries to fix everything that is 'wrong' within the family, even if such actions actually do the opposite. Sometimes, this can lead to smothering or being over-protective of the person with anorexia.

- **The People Pleaser:** This person lives to please others; ultimately, over time, the family member becomes unable to recognise their own needs and desires. This is often a trait found in the person with anorexia, but can also be present in other family members, leading to an enmeshment of needs — many of which remain unmet.

- **The Non-Feeler:** This family member, or members, choose to live in denial, refusing to accept that there is problem. Eventually, this person will become cold and unable to recognise or feel their own emotions. They also give the message that to have or express feelings is wrong. This can be particularly unhelpful for the person recovering from anorexia, where emotional expression is an important goal of long-term recovery.

Being open to exploring your role within the family will help you to make certain changes that might assist your loved one in their recovery. Again, this isn't about blame. It is about uniting as a family to beat anorexia.

## Family Rules

Not only do all families have roles, they also have rules — often unspoken — that define how the family operates. These can be broken down into family domains:

- **Fantasies:** What fantasies play out within the family? Examples of fantasies include 'We all stick together' or 'It's us against the world.'

- **Feelings:** As a 'rule', what emotions typify your family? Perhaps you are always happy and certain feelings, such as sadness or anger, aren't supposed to be expressed?

- **Boundaries:** Are the boundaries within your family open or closed? For example, is there an unspoken rule that everything that happens within the family stays within the family?

- **Authority:** Who has power within the family or does power change depending on the issue at hand?

These family rules become 'just the way things are done' and are rarely questioned. That is fine. There is nothing wrong with having rules; they help us function and add some order to our lives. However, when one family member becomes ill or doesn't appear to be functioning within these family dynamics, it is important to explore if any changes might be needed.

In a family where someone has anorexia, a shift in rules could help with recovery. For example, the idea that 'It's us against the world' (*fantasy*) might need to be changed in order for your loved one to gain trust in a health professional, and the belief that one always has to express happiness (*feelings*) might need to be changed in order for your loved one to learn how to express their feelings around the anorexia. Closed boundaries will need to change so your loved one can seek outside support (*boundaries*), and it might be necessary for some authority to be passed to your loved one so that they feel more in control of the recovery process (*authority*).

Take some time to think about your own family rules and how these could be used to help both your loved one and yourself.

# Chapter 14

# Be a Dolphin for Your Loved One

> " If you light a lamp for somebody, it will also brighten your path.
>
> Gautama Buddha "

As someone who cares for a loved one with anorexia, you will have your own way of coping with the fear and uncertainty of their illness. In turn, this will affect the way you react to your loved one. Let's take a closer look at your reactions and coping strategies so that you can start to establish what works and what doesn't.

## Responding to My Loved One

Take a piece of paper and create two columns, as shown below – one titled 'Reaction' and the other 'Outcome'. Identify the ways in which you respond to your loved one when their eating disorder rears its head. Do you get angry at them? Smother them? Treat them like a child? Start to write a list of all the ways you have reacted in the past, circling those that you feel are your most common reactions. What was the outcome of this reaction?

| Reaction | Outcome |
|---|---|
| e.g. I shouted at her to 'Just snap out of it and eat!' | e.g. She shouted back and stormed off. |
|  |  |

The eating disorder expert, Janet Treasure, uses animal metaphors to describe six types of carer.[1] Using the list of reactions you have just created, which metaphor best suits your coping style?

- **Kangaroo:** If you are a Kangaroo, you keep your loved one sheltered in your pouch in order to protect them. You see them as fragile and want to keep them out of harm's way.

- **Rhino:** If you are a Rhino, you tend to charge in with anger and frustration when your loved one's anorexia symptoms are present.

- **Dolphin:** A dolphin will gently nudge their loved one into safety, sometimes swimming ahead and leading in order to provide encouragement and support, and sometimes staying back so that their loved one can make their own way.

## Finding Balanced Coping

Being over-protective can be disabling, preventing your loved one from developing their own coping skills. Being angry or aggressive will simply lead your loved one to argue back, in favour of the anorexia. It is believed that the most helpful approach to recovery from anorexia is the dolphin, gently nudging your loved one towards recovery at a speed they are comfortable with.

Taking these animal metaphors further, which of the following best describes your emotional response to your loved one's anorexia?[2]

- **Ostrich:** If you are an Ostrich, you put your head in the sand, protecting yourself from your loved one's condition; it is just too distressing for you.

- **Jellyfish:** You are emotional and easily reduced to tears by the anorexia-related behaviours, blaming yourself for the illness.

- **St Bernard Dog:** A St Bernard Dog is reliable and consistent, staying calm in all situations. They also provide companionship.

## Finding Balanced Emotional Responses

Putting your head in the sand and showing too little emotion is likely to create a void between you and your loved one, while being too emotional could prevent you getting close to your loved one and being able to discuss important issues. Trying to emulate the St Bernard Dog, however, will provide you and your loved one with the opportunity to work together towards recovery.

There is no doubt that anorexia recovery is an emotional rollercoaster for all involved. If you are ever in doubt about the best way to be with your loved one's illness or recovery, stick to the three Cs:

- **Be calm:** Your loved one has a 'storm' going on inside and the more calmness displayed by those around them, the more chance they have of establishing enough stability to move forward with recovery.

- **Be consistent:** Send your loved one consistent messages in terms of the amount and level of support you can provide. The anorexia is looking for inconsistencies that it can use to remain in your loved one's life. Consistency will also help your loved one feel safe, which can eventually lead to taking more steps towards positive change.

- **Be compassionate:** Your loved one is already hurting enough. Show compassion for their struggles, so that they can learn to be compassionate with themselves. This won't always be easy. Sometimes you will find it very difficult to understand why they are doing this to themselves, but remind yourself that this is their way of coping with something that seems more painful than the anorexia itself.

Most importantly, never blame your loved one for their condition or tell them to 'snap out of it'. They are doing the best they can to cope with life and need your help to learn new ways of coping. There will be times you do feel angry at them, but try to walk away until things have calmed down and everyone is ready to talk — remember the importance of communication in anorexia recovery. Listen to your loved one when they do communicate — this is a big step for them. Don't listen to respond, but listen to understand. This will help you as well.

## Seeking Support for Yourself

We have explored how you can support your loved one, but there is no shame in also seeking support for yourself. It is important not to neglect your own needs and to acknowledge that your loved one's anorexia has an emotional impact on you. Counselling can be a useful coping tool, providing you with a place to voice any problems you are having and enabling you to find potential solutions. You will find a list of information and support services in the appendix. Equally, don't forgot to provide yourself with time away from the situation, alone or with friends, where you can relax and take part in activities you enjoy. There is no need to stop living your life, and the better you are coping, the stronger you can be for your loved one.

Another way you can support yourself is to read the rest of this book. While the content is for the person with anorexia, it will provide you with an in-depth insight into your loved one's world and the tools and techniques they are implementing in their efforts to recover. It will equip you to support them in this journey and prepare you for the road ahead.

# Resources for Eating Disorder Support and Recovery

## UK
••••

### Anorexia & Bulimia Care (ABC)

ABC provides ongoing care, emotional support and practical guidance for those with eating disorders.

www.anorexiabulimiacare.org.uk

### Beat – Beating Eating Disorders

Beat provides support and information for both adolescents and adults with eating disorders, including online and email services.

www.b-eat.co.uk

### Beat – Live Chat Support Forum

Beat's online service allows you to talk to others who are in a similar situation in a safe environment in real time.

www.b-eat.co.uk/support-services/online-support-groups

### Men Get Eating Disorders Too

This organisation offers support to men with eating disorders, as well as to their carers and families.

http://mengetedstoo.co.uk

## National Centre for Eating Disorders (NCFED)

The NCFED offers information and counselling for those with eating disorders from specialised counsellors.

http://eating-disorders.org.uk

## National Health Services (NHS) Choices

The NHS provides the facts about eating disorders, including what they are, who is affected by them and what to do if you need help.

www.nhs.uk/Livewell/eatingdisorders/Pages/eatingdisordershomepage.aspx

## Royal College of Psychiatrists (RCP)

The RCP offers well-researched, yet easy-to-understand, information about eating disorders.

www.rcpsych.ac.uk/mentalhealthinfo/problems/eatingdisorders/eatingdisorders.aspx

## SEED – Eating Disorder Support Services

SEED offers services via online, phone, email, groups, workshops, self-help and advice-giving.

www.seedeatingdisorders.org.uk/services

# Ireland

## Bodywhys – The Eating Disorders Association of Ireland

Bodywhys, the Irish national support association for those with eating disorders, provides a website detailing services available in the area.

www.bodywhys.ie

# Appendix

## Example Relapse Prevention Plan

| My Relapse Prevention Plan | | | | |
|---|---|---|---|---|
| **What are the high-risk situations or triggers that I need to be mindful of?** <br> *e.g.* <br> *Gaining weight* <br> *Stress with treatment* <br> *Magazines* <br> *Social events* <br> *Shopping for new clothes* | **My life beyond anorexia** <br> I want to stay on track with my recovery. Here's a list to remind me of my long-term life improvement goals: <br> Personal development: Build my self-confidence <br> Career: I want to be a teacher <br> Health: Have a more varied diet <br> Education: Teacher training <br> Relationships: Spend more time with my best friend <br> Creativity: Start painting | | | |
| **What warning signals/lapses have I had?** | **Which area of my well-being is affected?** | **What is the possible trigger?** | **Which tool do I plan to use?*** | **Which chapter should I review?** |
| e.g. Purging | Behavioural/ Physical | A social event with food | Practise 15-minute rule, making a distraction list | Chapter 6 |
| e.g. Intensifying exercise and doing it in solitude | Behavioural/ Physical | Seeing friends who diet/exercise | Join exercise groups that promote body appreciation | Chapter 7 |
| e.g. Feeling 'fat' | Emotional | Magazines | Write feelings down in a mood diary | Chapter 8 |
| e.g. Feeling pessimistic about treatment | Emotional | Shopping for new clothes | Put together a jar of motivation for remaining healthy | Chapter 6, Chapter 11 |
| e.g. Revisiting pro-anorexia websites | Cognitive | Gaining weight | STOPP strategy, Counter-belief statements | Chapter 5, Chapter 8, Chapter 10 |
| e.g. Withdrawal from other people | Social | Stress with treatment | Speak with a recovery buddy | Chapter 6, Chapter 9 |
| Here is a list of individuals I can get in touch with if ever I need additional support: | | | | |
| **Healthcare professionals** | **Family members** | | **Friends** | |
| My GP | My sister | | Sharon (emotional support) | |
| My counsellor | My auntie | | Gail (fun) | |

# Relapse Prevention Plan Template

| My Relapse Prevention Plan | |
|---|---|
| **What are the high-risk situations or triggers that I need to be mindful of?** | **My life beyond anorexia**<br>I want to stay on track with my recovery. Here's a list to remind me of my long-term life improvement goals.<br><br>Personal Development:<br><br><br><br>Career:<br><br><br><br>Health:<br><br><br><br>Education:<br><br><br><br>Relationships:<br><br><br><br>Creativity: |

| What warning signals/lapses have I had? | Which area of my well-being is affected? (behavioural, physical, social, emotional or cognitive) | What is the possible trigger? | Which tool do I plan to use?* | Which chapter should I review? |
|---|---|---|---|---|
|  |  |  |  |  |
|  |  |  |  |  |
|  |  |  |  |  |
|  |  |  |  |  |
|  |  |  |  |  |

| Here is a list of individuals I can get in touch with if ever I need additional support: | | |
|---|---|---|
| Healthcare professionals | Family members | Friends |
|  |  |  |
|  |  |  |

*Throughout reading this book, you've come across several tools to help you begin and maintain recovery. Here is a summary of the tools you can select from when developing and using your relapse prevention plan:

**Chapter 3**
Seeking information
Seeking assistance
Finding belonging
Seeking emotional support
Asking for feedback
Finding relief

**Chapter 4**
Counselling
Inner child work

**Chapter 5**
Mastery experiences
Vicarious experiences
Self-persuasion
Experiencing positive physiological states

**Chapter 6**
Self-soothing
Food diary
Adaptive/intuitive eating
Distraction list
15-minute rule
Motivational jar

**Chapter 7**
Determining hunger type
Selecting exercise for health
Appreciating the body for what it does

**Chapter 8**
Mood diary
Thought record
STOPP strategy
Using counter-beliefs
Emotion-focused therapy

**Chapter 9**
Spending time in positive relationships
Breaking free from family roles

**Chapter 10**
Self-acceptance
Observing self from a distance
Affirmations
Self-acknowledgement

# Notes

## Chapter 1

1. American Psychiatric Association (2013) *Diagnostic and Statistical Manual of Mental Disorders, Fifth Edition*. Arlington, VA: American Psychiatric Association.
2. Priory Group (2016) 'Eating Disorder Statistics.' Available at www.priorygroup.com/eating-disorders/statistics (accessed 29 November 2016).
3. NHS Choices (2016) 'Anorexia Nervosa – Diagnosis.' Available at www.nhs.uk/Conditions/anorexia-nervosa/Pages/diagnosis.aspx (accessed 29 November 2016).
4. Bonci, C.M., Bonci, L.J., Granger, L.R., Johnson, C.L., Malina, R.M., Milne, L.W. et al. (2008) 'National Athletic Trainers' Association position statement: Preventing, detecting, and managing disordered eating in athletes.' *Journal of Athletic Training* 43, 1, 80–108.
5. Baker, J. (2015) 'The Genetic Risk for Eating Disorders and the Anorexia Nervosa Genetics Initiative.' Mirror Mirror Eating Disorders. Available at www.mirror-mirror.org/genetics-and-eating-disorders.htm (accessed 29 November 2016).
6. Barker, S. and Ahn, B. (2016) 'Causal factors of eating disorder behaviors in adolescent females.' *Undergraduate Research Journal for the Human Sciences 15*, 1. Available at www.kon.org/urc/v15/barker.html (accessed 22 January 2017).
7. Madowitz, J., Matheson, B.E. and Liang, J. (2015) 'The relationship between eating disorders and sexual trauma.' *Eating and Weight Disorders – Studies on Anorexia, Bulimia and Obesity 20*, 3, 281–293.
8. Thornton, L.M., Welch, E., Munn-Chernoff, M.A., Lichtenstein, P. and Bulik, C.M. (2016) 'Anorexia nervosa, major depression, and suicide attempts: Shared genetic factors.' *Suicide and Life-Threatening Behavior 46*, 5, 525–534.
9. Wimmer-Puchinger, B., Blahout, S. and Waldherr, K. (2016) 'Eating disorders: What has the society to do with it?' *European Psychiatry 33*, S167.

## Chapter 2

1. Office of Women's Health (2012) 'Anorexia Nervosa Fact Sheet.' Available at www.womenshealth.gov/publications/our-publications/fact-sheet/anorexia-nervosa.html (accessed 29 November 2016).
2. National Collaborating Centre for Mental Health (2004) *Eating Disorders: Core Interventions in the Treatment and Management of Anorexia Nervosa, Bulimia Nervosa and Related Eating Disorders*. National Clinical Practice Guideline Number CG9. Leicester and London: British Psychological Society and Royal College of Psychiatrists.

# Chapter 3

1. Troscianko, E. (2015) 'Recovering from anorexia: How and why to start.' Psychology Today. Available at www.psychologytoday.com/blog/hunger-artist/201501/recovering -anorexia-how-and-why-start (accessed 30 December 2016).

2. Australian Associated Press (AAP) (2011) 'Anorexics lack sense of belonging, study finds.' Available at www.news.com.au/breaking-news/anorexics-lack-sense-of-belonging/story-e6frfku0- 1226121438873 (accessed 30 December 2016).

3. American Psychological Association (2011) 'Eating Disorders.' Available at www.apa. org/helpcenter/eating.aspx (accessed 29 November 2016).

4. Gleissner, G. (2016) 'Eating disorder recovery: Five things to consider in your post-treatment plan.' *Huffington Post.* Available at www.huffingtonpost.com/greta-gleissner/ eating-disorder-recovery-_b_ 10283206.html (accessed 29 November 2016).

# Chapter 4

1. Shostorm, E. and Brammer, L. (1952) *The Dynamics of the Counseling Process.* New York: McGraw. Cited in Kumar, S. (2015) 'What are the basic principles and characteristics of counselling?' Available at www.publishyourarticles.net/knowledge-hub/education/ what-are-the-basic-principles-and-characteristics-of-counselling/5379 (accessed 29 November 2016).

2. Counselling Directory (2016) 'Anorexia Nervosa.' Available at www.counselling-directory.org.uk/anorexia.html (accessed 29 November 2016).

3. NHS Choices (2014) 'Counselling.' Available at www.nhs.uk/conditions/Counselling/ Pages/Introduction.aspx (accessed 29 November 2016).

4. Bell, L. (2015) 'Interpersonal therapy for treatment of bulimia.' Eating Disorder Hope. Available at www.eatingdisorderhope.com/blog/interpersonal-therapy-for-treatment-of-bulimia (accessed 29 November 2016).

5. NHS Choices (2014) 'Counselling.' Available at www.nhs.uk/conditions/Counselling/ Pages/Introduction.aspx (accessed 29 November 2016).

# Chapter 5

1. Schade, R. (2016) *Silent Kingdom.* ASTA Publications LLC.

2. Prochaska, J.O., DiClemente, C.C. and Norcross, J.C. (1992) 'In search of how people change: Applications to addictive behavior.' *American Psychologist 47*, 1102–1114.

3. Giannini, A.J. and Slaby, A.E. (eds) (2012) *The Eating Disorders.* New York: Springer Science & Business Media.

4. Eating Disorders Institute of New Mexico (2015) 'Whistle a happy tune – Sources of self-efficacy.' *Eating Disorders Quarterly 6*, 1, 3. Available at www.eating disordersnm.com/wp-content/uploads/2014/12/Newsletter_2015_Q1.pdf (accessed 30 December 2016).

5. Karges, C. (n.d.) 'Body image and self-talk: Do affirmations help?' Eating Disorder Hope. Available at www.eatingdisorderhope.com/information/body-image/body-image-and-self-talk-do-affirmations-help (accessed 29 November 2016).

6. Agency for Healthcare Research and Quality (2014) 'Community Connections.' Available at www.ahrq.gov/professionals/prevention-chronic-care/improve/community/obesity-toolkit/obtoolkit-tool14.html (accessed 29 November 2016).

# Chapter 6

1.  Ekern, J. (2016) 'Effective coping skills: Eating disorder self-soothing.' Eating Disorder Hope. Available at www.eatingdisorderhope.com/recovery/self-help-tools-skills-tips/self-soothing-advice (accessed 29 November 2016).
2.  Getselfhelp (2016) Food Diary. Available at www.getselfhelp.co.uk/docs/FoodDiary2.pdf (accessed 29 November 2016)
3.  Department of Health (2011) 'Physical activity guidelines for adults (19–64 years).' Available at http://www.nhs.uk/Livewell/fitness/Documents/adults-19-64-years.pdf (accessed 29 March 2017).

# Chapter 7

1.  Arnold, C. (2013) 'The Other Side of Hunger Cues: Fullness Cues.' ED Bites. Available at http://edbites.com/2013/07/the-other-side-of-hunger-cues-fullness-cues (accessed 29 November 2016).
2.  Koenigsberger, D. and Fortney, L. (2010). *Mindful Eating: Discovering a Better Relationship with Your Food.* Available at www.fammed.wisc.edu/files/webfm-uploads/documents/outreach/im/handout_mindful_eating.pdf (accessed 29 November 2016).
3.  Weltzin, T. (2012). 'Causes, Diagnosis & Treatment Options of Excessive Exercise.' Eating Disorder Hope. Available at www.eatingdisorderhope.com/information/orthorexia-excessive-exercise/diagnosis-evaluation-causes-treatment (accessed 29 November 2016).
4.  Cook, B.J., Wonderlich, S., Mitchell, J., Thompson, R., Sherman, R. and McCallum, K. (2016) 'Exercise in eating disorders treatment: Systematic review and proposal of guidelines.' *Medicine and Science in Sports and Exercise 48*, 7, 1408–1414.
5.  Carei, T., Fyfe-Johnson, A., Breuner, C. and Marshall, M. (2010) 'Randomized controlled clinical trial of yoga in the treatment of eating disorders.' *Journal of Adolescent Health 46*, 4, 346–351.
6.  Weltzin 2012.
7.  Olwyn, G. (2012) 'Phases of recovery from a restrictive eating disorder.' The Eating Disorder Institute. Available at www.youreatopia.com/blog/2012/11/23/phases-of-recovery-from-a-restrictive-eating-disorder.html (accessed 29 November 2016).

# Chapter 8

1.  Rowsell, M., Macdonald, D. and Carter, J. (2016) 'Emotion regulation difficulties in anorexia nervosa: Associations with improvements in eating psychopathology.' *Journal of Eating Disorders 4*, 17.
2.  Ioannou, K. and Fox, J. (2009) 'Perception of threat from emotions and its role in poor emotional expression within eating pathology.' *Clinical Psychology and Psychotherapy 16*, 4, 336–347.
3.  Rowsell, MacDonald and Carter 2016.
4.  Fedrici, A. (2004) 'Relapse and recovery in anorexia nervosa: The patients' perspective.' Proquest Digital Dissertations, ID#845748931.
5.  Dolhanty, J. (2006) 'Emotion-focused therapy for eating disorders.' NEDIC. Available at http://nedic.ca/emotion-focused-therapy-eating-disorders (accessed 29 November 2016).
6.  Murphy, R., Straebler, S., Cooper, Z. and Fairburn, C. (2010) 'Cognitive behavioral therapy for eating disorders.' *Psychiatric Clinics of North America 33*, 3, 611–627.

7.   Selby, E. (2014) 'Anorexia Nervosa and Positive Emotion.' Psychology Today. Available at www.psychologytoday.com/blog/overcoming-self-sabotage/201408/anorexia-nervosa-and-positive-emotion (accessed 29 November 2016).

8.   Emotion-Focused Therapy Clinic (2016) 'What is Emotion-Focused Therapy?' Available at www.emotionfocusedclinic.org/whatis.htm (accessed 29 November 2016).

9.   Ekern, J. (2016) 'Feelings & eating disorders recovery.' Eating Disorder Hope. Available at www.eatingdisorderhope.com/recovery/self-help-tools-skills-tips/feelings (accessed 29 November 2016).

10.  Vivyan, C. (2010) Mood Diary. Available at www.getselfhelp.co.uk/docs/MoodDiary2.pdf (accessed 29 November 2016).

11.  Getselfhelp (2016) Available at http://get.gg/docs/MoodDiary.pdf (accessed 29 November 2016).

12.  Ekern, J. (2012) 'Overcoming negative thoughts from eating disorders.' Eating Disorder Hope. Available at www.eatingdisorderhope.com/recovery/self-help-tools-skills-tips/overcome-negative-thinking (accessed 29 November 2016).

13.  Grohol, J. (2015) '15 common cognitive distortions.' Psych Central. Available at http://psychcentral.com/lib/15-common-cognitive-distortions (accessed 29 November 2016).

14.  Ekern 2012.

15.  Grohol 2015.

16.  Murphy et al. 2010.

17.  Vivyan, C. (2009) Thought Record Sheet – Anorexia. Available at http://get.gg/docs/AnorexiaThoughtRecordSheet.pdf (accessed 29 November 2016).

18.  NHS Choices (2016) 'Cognitive behavioural therapy (CBT).' Available at www.nhs.uk/conditions/Cognitive-behavioural-therapy/Pages/Introduction.aspx (accessed 29 November 2016).

19.  Murphy et al. 2010.

# Chapter 9

1.   Somenah, K. (2013) 'Relationship skills for those in eating disorder recovery.' Eating Disorder Hope. Available at www.eatingdisorderhope.com/recovery/self-help-tools-skills-tips/relationship-skills-for-those-in-eating-disorder-recovery (accessed 29 November 2016).

2.   WebMD (2014) 'Eating Disorders: Cultural and Social Factors – Topic Overview.' Available at www.webmd.com/mental-health/eating-disorders/tc/eating-disorders-cultural-and-social-factors-topic-overview (accessed 29 November 2016).

3.   Thompson, L. and McCabe, R. (2015) '"Good" Communication in Schizophrenia: A Conversation Analytic Definition.' In O'Reilly, M. and Lester, J.N. (eds) The Palgrave Handbook of Child Mental Health (pp.394–418). Basingstoke: Palgrave Macmillan.

4.   Engel, B., Staats Reiss, N. and Dombeck, M. (2016) 'Causes of Eating Disorders – Family Influences.' Behavioural Connections. Available at www.behavioralconnections.org/poc/view_doc.php?type=doc&id=11751&cn=46 (accessed 29 November 2016).

5.   Engel, Staats Reiss and Dombeck 2016.

6.   Engel, Staats Reiss and Dombeck 2016.

7.   Bowen, M. (1978) Family Therapy In Clinical Practice. New York: Aronson.

8. University of Haifa (2011) 'Facebook users more prone to developing eating disorders, study finds.' ScienceDaily. Available at www.sciencedaily.com/releases/2011/02/110207091754.htm (accessed 29 November 2016).

9. Health Talk (2015) 'Friends and Relationships.' Available at www.healthtalk.org/young-peoples-experiences/eating-disorders/friends-and-relationships#ixzz4GuehONhJ (accessed 29 November 2016).

10. Dunkerley, S. (2014) *Close Relationships and Eating Disorder Recovery: Partner Perspectives*. Thesis. Available at https://ttu-ir.tdl.org/ttu-ir/bitstream/handle/2346/58512/DUNKERLEY-THESIS-2014.pdf?sequence=1 (accessed 29 November 2016).

11. Carter, S. (2011) 'The hidden health hazards of toxic relationships.' Psychology Today. Available at www.psychologytoday.com/blog/high-octane-women/201108/the-hidden-health-hazards-toxic-relationships (accessed 29 November 2016).

12. Labrie, C. (2015) 'Repairing broken friendships in eating disorder recovery.' Eating Disorder Hope. Available at www.eatingdisorderhope.com/treatment-for-eating-disorders/special-issues/families/repairing-broken-friendships-in-eating-disorder-recovery (accessed 29 November 2016).

# Chapter 10

1. Kilinger, D. (2010) 'The role of self-acceptance in recovering from eating disorders.' GoodTherapy.org. Available at http://www.goodtherapy.org/blog/therapy-eating-self-esteem (accessed 30 December 2016).

2. Kilinger 2010.

# Chapter 11

1. Baumann, M. (2007) 'Life during recovery: Questions to ask yourself.' National Eating Disorders Association (NEDA). Available at www.nationaleatingdisorders.org/life-during-recovery-questions-ask-yourself (accessed 29 November 2016).

2. Morand, M. (2011) 'Setting reasonable goals for eating disorders recovery.' Available at www.eatingdisorderhope.com/recovery/self-help-tools-skills-tips/goal-setting (accessed 29 November 2016).

3. Thompson, C. (2014) 'Eating Disorder Relapse Prevention.' Mirror Mirror Eating disorders. Available at www.mirror-mirror.org/relprev.htm (accessed 29 November 2016).

# Chapter 13

1. Bowen, M. (1978) *Family Therapy In Clinical Practice*. New York: Aronson.

# Chapter 14

1. Treasure, J., Smith, G. and Crane, A. (2007) *Skills-Based Caring for a Loved One with an Eating Disorder: The New Maudsley Model*. Abingdon: Routledge.

2. Treasure, Smith and Crane 2007.

**Dr Nicola Davies** is a health psychologist, counsellor, and medical writer specialising in raising awareness about health and wellbeing. She is a member of the British Psychological Society and the British Association for Counselling and Psychotherapy. Nicola also keeps a health psychology blog and runs an online forum for counsellors. She struggled with eating disorders from childhood into her 30s and wants to help others break free from an unhealthy relationship with food and weight. Nicola is the author of *I Can Beat Obesity!* (ISBN 9781785921537) and the co-author of the *Eating Disorder Recovery Handbook* (ISBN 9781785921339), also published by Jessica Kingsley Publishers.